Generis
PUBLISHING

Imbalances of Body Minerals in Children with Autism

Hiroshi Yasuda

Title: Imbalances of Body Minerals in Children with Autism

ISBN: 979-8-89248-533-3

Author: Hiroshi Yasuda

Cover image: www.pixabay.com

Publisher: Generis Publishing
Online orders: www.generis-publishing.com
Contact email: info@generis-publishing.com

Contents

Introduction

The prevalence of children with neurodevelopmental disorders such as autism spectrum disorders (ASD) and attention-deficit/hyper activity disorder (ADHD) has been increasing during recent decades. For instance, autistic disorders are identified in children at a rate of 1 in 50. Therefore, elucidation of the etiology and effective treatment of neurodevelopmental disorders is an urgent problem and one of the challenges today.

The seven research articles collected in this book call attention to the deficiency of only two trace elements "zinc and magnesium" among 13 essential minerals and also to the high burdens of toxic metals such as aluminum, lead, cadmium, and mercury or arsenic, especially in the 0-3 years old infants with neurodevelopmental disorders. These findings indicate that the presence of a critical period named "Infantile Time Window" in the pathogenesis of neurodevelopmental disorders and for the treatment, suggesting that the early assessment and intervention of the body mineral imbalances in the patients are essential for the prevention and therapy.

In **Chapter 1,** Yasuda et al (2011) published the first article on a series of metallomics study for 1,967 autistic children (1,533 males and 414 females aged 0-15 years), in which an essential mineral zinc element in scalp hair sample was examined and demonstrated that 584 subjects (29.7%) are suffered from zinc-deficiency. In particular, the rate of zinc-deficiency in infant group aged 0-3 years was estimated 43.5% in mail and 52.5% in female. These findings suggest that infantile zinc-deficiency epigenetically contributes to the pathogenesis of autism and that nutritional approach may yield a novel hope for its prevention and treatment.

In **Chapter 2,** We examine scalp hair concentrations of 26 trace elements for 1,967 children with autistic disorders. Five-hundred and eighty-four (29.7%), 347 (17.6%) and 114 (5.8%) individuals is found deficient in zinc, magnesium and calcium, respectively, and 2.0% or less in the other essential metals such as iron or copper. The incidence rate of zinc deficiency reaches about 50% in the infants aged 0-3 years. In addition, 339 (17.2%), 168 (8.5%) and 94 (4.8%) individuals are suffered from high burden of aluminum, cadmium and lead, and 2.8% or less from mercury and arsenic burden. These findings suggest that infantile zinc- and magnesium-deficiency and/or toxic metal burdens seem epigenetically play principal roles as environmental factors in autistic disorders and that metallomics approach leads to early screening and prevention of the neurodevelopmental disorders.

In **Chapter 3,** Yasuda and Tsutsui review the findings in the metallomics studies for the 1,967 autistic children (1,533 males and 414 females aged 0-15 years) and discuss recent advances in our understanding on the epigenetic roles of infantile various mineral imbalances, "zinc- and magnesium-deficiency and high burdens of toxic metals", in the etiology of ASD and ADHD. Typical some metallome profiles of the individuals suffering from various mineral imbalances such as severe zinc- and magnesium-deficiency, toxic metal burdens or sodium/potassium imbalance are visualized.

Thus, clinical metallomics analysis is expected useful for early assessment, diagnosis and intervention/therapy of the children with neurodevelopmental disorders.

In **Chapter 4,** Another metallomics study article reported by Yasuda, Tsutsui and Suzuki (2022), "**Metallomics analysis for assessment of toxic metal burdens in infants/children and their mothers: Early assessment and intervention are essential.**" for a volunteer group of 77 child/mother pairs, is cited. Mercury concentration in children was of similar level to that in their mothers, and a high-significant close correlation was observed between children and their mothers. For lead, cadmium and aluminum, their mean accumulation levels in children were approximately three times higher than those in their mothers, and their burden levels in some individuals, especially in infants, were several tens of times higher than in their mothers. In contrast, some essential metals such as zinc and magnesium were significantly lower than those in their mothers, and 29 individuals (37.7%) of the child subjects were estimated zinc-deficient. In addition, significant inverse correlations between zinc and lead ($r = -0.267$, $p = 0.019$) and between magnesium and arsenic ($r = -0.514$, $p = 0.0001$) were observed in children. High burdens of toxic metals and deficiency of the antagonistic essential metals in infants are of serious concern, and so, early assessment and intervention of such individuals would be helpful for their normal neurodevelopment and health.

In **Chapter 5,** A recent perspective article "**Metallomics analysis for early assessment and individualized intervention of neurodevelopmental disorders**", based on the metallomics study for total 2,550 autistic children, is presented.

This review article shows recent advances based on the metallomics studies for the pathogenesis of neurodevelopmental disorders, and summarizes the decisive evidences, namely "Epigenetic Mechanism Induced by Infantile/fetal Zinc- and Magnesium-Deficiency and not only Toxic Metals' Burdens but also some Essential Metals' Overloads". We expect that early assessment and intervention of the various mineral imbalances (or dis-homeostasis) in individual child open an avenue for evidence-based individualized therapy of neurodevelopmental disorders and also of the comorbid immune disorders, in near future.

Supplement

Chapter 6. "Two age-related accumulation profiles of toxic metals"

Five toxic metal concentrations in scalp hair samples from 28,424 Japanese subjects from infant to elderly were determined with ICP-MS. Hair mercury concentration showed a high-significant age-correlated increase ($r = 0.341$, $p < 0.0001$) with a peak at the 6th decade of life and then decreased with further aging in both sexes. The mean mercury concentration in male adults were significantly higher than those in female ($p < 0.001$), indicating the gender difference (male > female) in mercury accumulation. Arsenic also showed a similar accumulation profile to mercury, with age-dependency and gender difference in adults. In contrast, cadmium, lead and aluminum exhibited another type of accumulation profile: the highest burden level was observed in infants aged 0-3 years old for every element in both sexes. In addition, cadmium was found to have a character accumulating in aged females, with age dependency ($r = 0.134$, $p < 0.0001$) and gender difference (female > male). These findings suggest that toxic metals are classified into two families on the basis of their accumulation profiles, and that the three elements of mercury, arsenic and cadmium which accumulate age-dependently in adults, may play a role in aging process and higher burden with them may lead to acceleration of aging. Further understanding of molecular and cellular mechanisms of aging could not only improve medical care of the elderly but also hold out some hope in finding feasible solutions to slow down the aging process.

Chapter 7. "Infants and elderlies are susceptible to zinc deficiency."

The importance of zinc for human health has been recognized since the early 1960s, but today there is little concern about zinc deficiency in developed countries. In this study, we measured the zinc concentration in hair from 28,424 Japanese subjects (18,812 females and 9,612 males) and found that 1,754 individuals (6.17%) had zinc concentrations lower than -2 standard deviation level (86.3 ppm) in the reference range, which qualifies as zinc deficiency. The prevalence of zinc deficiency in adults increase with aging to a maximum of

19.7% by the 8th decade of life, and decrease to 3.4% above 90-year-old dramatically. The proportion of zinc deficiency in infants 0–4 years was 36.5% in males and 47.3% in females. These findings suggest that not only infants but also elderlies are prone to zinc deficiency and that early intervention of zinc deficiency is necessary for normal human development, health and longevity.

Chapter 1 :

INFANTILE ZINC DEFICIENCY: ASSOCIATION WITH AUTISM SPECTRUM DISORDERS (as Key Epigenetic Factor)

published in **Scientific Reports 1: 129 (2011).**

Hiroshi Yasuda[1], Kazuya Yoshida[1], Yuichi Yasuda[2] & Toyoharu Tsutsui[1]
[1]La Belle Vie Research Laboratory, Tokyo 103-0006, Japan, [2]Health Science Laboratory, Tokyo, Japan.

Abstract: Elucidation of the pathogenesis and effective treatment of autism spectrum disorders is one of the challenges today. In this study, we examine hair zinc concentrations for 1,967 children with autistic disorders (1,553 males and 414 females), and show considerable association with zinc deficiency. Histogram of hair zinc concentration was non-symmetric with tailing in lower range, and 584 subjects were found to have lower zinc concentrations than 22 standard deviation level of its reference range (86.3–193 ppm). The incidence rate of zinc deficiency in infant group aged 0–3 years-old was estimated 43.5 % in male and 52.5 % in female. The lowest zinc concentration of 10.7 ppm was detected in a 2-year-old boy, corresponding to about 1/12 of the control mean level. These findings suggest that infantile zinc deficiency may epigenetically contribute to the pathogenesis of autism and nutritional approach may yield a novel hope for its treatment and prevention.

Autism spectrum disorders are a group of neural development disorders characterized by impairments in reciprocal social interaction and communication, and by the presence of restricted and repetitive behaviors[1], affecting 1 in 150 children in developed countries[2]. Therefore, the elucidation of the pathogenesis and effective treatment of autistic disorders is one of the challenges today. Autism spectrum disorders is thought to be heritable and some related genes have been reported[3,4]. However, the underlying genetic determinants are still unclarified[1] and the interaction of heritable factors with uncertified lifestyle and environmental factors seem play a significant role in the pathogenesis. For example, ethyl-mercury, a component in vaccines has been claimed to be one of the environmental candidates causing autistic disorders[5], but its relationship with autism remains to be proved scientifically.

Recently, epigenetic alteration of gene expression by environmental influences is considered one of key events in the pathogenesis of genetic diseases[6]. And some toxic elements such as cadmium, arsenic and mercury, and also essential mineral deficiencies have been reported to be candidate factors that induce epigenetic disorders[7–9].

Recent great advances in high-sensitive and reliable trace element analysis method using inductively coupled plasma mass spectrometry (ICP-MS) have enabled it to be applied for estimating chronic toxic metal burden and essential mineral deficiency in human body, showing that human blood mineral concentrations reflect to their levels in hair or nail specimen[10,11]. Thus, clinical metallomics studies with reliable ICP-MS method have been tried for investigating some association of several diseases and symptoms with the dynamics of trace bio-elements such as toxic metals and essential minerals[12–18].

The importance of zinc in human nutrition and health has been recognized since the early 1960s. For assessment of zinc nutritional status, the use of serum zinc alone is subject to limitations because its level seems be influenced by factors other than dietary zinc intake; for example, hypoalbuminemia, infection, acute stress, pregnancy and use of oral contraceptive agents can lower serum zinc values[19]. In addition, serum zinc levels are subject to diurnal variation and influenced by the fasting status of the subjects.

For the last five years, we have examined on the association of toxic metal burden with autistic disorders, and reported that some parts of the children with autism have suffered from high accumulation of toxic metals such as cadmium, lead or aluminium more than mercury[20–22].

In this preliminary study, we have determined human scalp hair zinc concentrations for 1,967 children diagnosed with autistic spectrum disorders by their physicians, and showed that many of them, especially in the infant group aged 0–3 year-old, are suffering from zinc deficiency.

Results

The histogram of logarithmic hair zinc concentrations for 1,967 children diagnosed with autism by their physicians is shown in Figure 1. The distribution of the logarithmic zinc concentration was non-symmetric with tailing in lower range, and 584 in 1,967 subjects (29.7 %) were found to have low zinc concentration less than -2 S.D. (standard deviation) level of the control reference range (86.3–193 micro g/g hair (ppm); geometric mean = 129 ppm), estimated as zinc deficiency. The logarithmic zinc concentrations in the autistic subjects showed a significant correlation with age ($r = 0.367$, $p < 0.0001$), with a plateau at over 10 years-old (Figure 2).

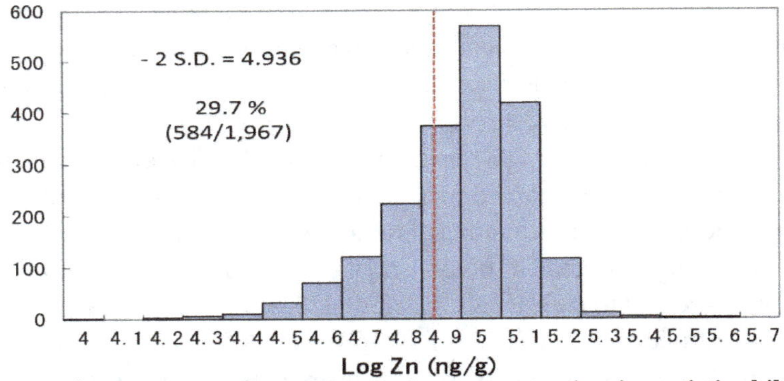

Figure 1 | Histogram of logarithmic zinc concentration in autistic children

The histogram of scalp hair zinc concentrations for 1,967 children (1,553 males and 414 females) aged 0–15 year-old is shown in the logarithm. The numbers on the abscissa indicate the logarithms of scalp hair zinc concentrations (ng/g hair: ppb). The height of each rectangle represents the frequency in the class interval in logarithmic hair zinc level. The dotted vertical line represents the -2 S.D. (standard deviation) level of the control reference range of hair zinc concentrations.

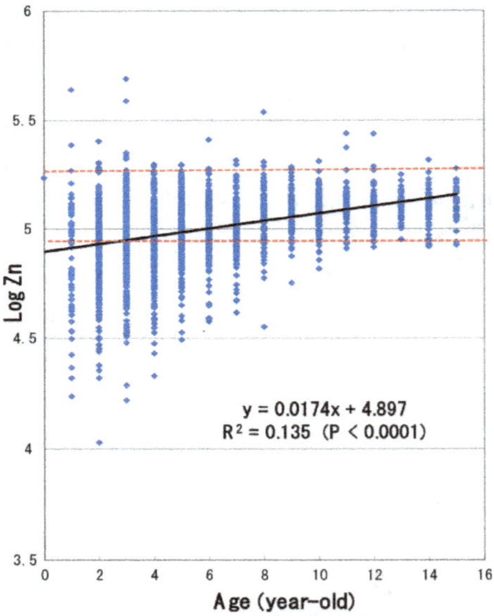

Figure 2. Age related increase in zinc concentration in autistic children

The association of hair logarithmic zinc concentration with age in autistic children (N = 1,967) is shown. Each spot represents the corresponding age and logarithmic zinc concentration of the respective child. A significant association of the zinc concentration with age ($r = 0.367$, $p < 0.0001$) in the autistic children is shown.

The only one 0-year-old case in 1,967 subjects was 11 month-old female with no zinc deficiency (Fig. 2) and may be a suspect, because she was found to suffer from high burdens with aluminium, lead, iron and copper (data not shown). The minimum zinc concentration of 10.7 ppm was observed in a 2-year-old boy, corresponding to about 1/12 of the control mean level. The geometric mean zinc concentration was lowest in the age group of 0–3 years-old in both sexes (Table 1).

Table 1 | Geometric mean zinc concentrations in autistic children

Gender	Age	No.	Mean Zn Level
Male	0–3 year–old	577	87
	4–9 year–old	736	100
	10–15 year–old	240	124
Female	0–3 year–old	118	81
	4–9 year–old	181	104
	10–15 year–old	115	131

The geometric mean zinc concentrations (ppm) in the age groups of 0–3, 4–9 and 10–15 years-old in 1,967 autistic children (1,553 males and 414 females) are tabled.

Table 2 | Incidence rate of zinc deficiency in autistic children

Gender	Age	No.	Number of Cases with Zn Deficiency	Rate (%) of Zn Deficiency
Male	0–3 year–old	577	251	43.5
	4–9 year–old	736	207	28.1
	10–15 year–old	240	8	3.3
Female	0–3 year–old	118	62	52.5
	4–9 year–old	181	52	28.7
	10–15 year–old	115	4	3.5

The number and incidence rate of the individuals with zinc deficiency in 1,967 autistic children (1,553 males and 414 females) are tabled.

The incidence rate of zinc deficiency in the age group of 0–3 and 4–9 years-old was estimated 43.5 and 28.1 % in male, and 52.5 and 28.7 % in female, respectively (Table 2). In the group aged 10–15 years-old, the zinc deficiency rate in male and female was calculated 3.3 and 3.5 %, respectively. There was little marked gender difference observed in scalp hair zinc concentration and incidence rate of zinc deficiency in the subjects with autism.

Discussion

Zinc is an essential trace element that plays important roles in nucleic acid/protein synthesis, cell replication, tissue growth and repair, especially in pregnant women and infants. Therefore, zinc deficiency is known associated with various pathological conditions, including impaired immunity, delayed wound healing, retarded growth, neural development disorders and degenerative diseases[23,24].

Hair zinc is commonly used in marginal zinc deficiency studies of children, and its usefulness has been documented in many industrialized countries including Canada and the USA[25–29]. In the present study, we determined zinc concentration in scalp hair samples from 1,967 subjects (1,553 males and 414 females) diagnosed with autism by physicians, and investigated any association of zinc deficiency with autistic spectrum disorders.

The control zinc reference range for healthy subjects published by ourselves[17,18] was almost consistent with those reported by other research groups[10–12] and those for nutritionally-controlled children reported by Munakata et al.[13] and Vancouver preschoolers aged 2–5 year-old (N = 719) by Vaghri et al.[28,29]. Based on these findings, the normal human hair zinc level was estimated to be around 130 ppm independently age and sex, although it was relatively low during childhood[19,28] (Fig. 2) and infants seem liable to fall into zinc deficiency because of their higher necessity of zinc for developing and growing. Thus, the lower zinc levels for control children reported by Adams et al.[15], Munakata et al.[13] and ourselves[14] should be re-considered as non-normal control values including non-healthy, affected zinc levels, as Adams themselves recently reviewed that the 11% participants in the neurotypical control children group were medicated with drugs such as anti-asthma/allergies or anti-incontinence[30].

The histogram of logarithmic hair zinc concentration in the 1,967 autistic children showed a non-symmetric profile with a marked tailing in lower range, indicating that about 30 % of the subjects with autism have low zinc concentrations less than -2 S.D. level (86.3 ppm) of the control reference range, being estimated as marginal zinc deficiency (Fig. 1). In particular, nearly one half (male: 43.5 %; female: 52.5 %) of the autistic infants aged 0–3 years-old were found to suffer from marginal to severe zinc deficiency (Table 2).

A significant correlation ($r = 0.367$, $p < 0.0001$) of the zinc concentration with age in the autistic subjects (Fig. 2) suggests that children, in particular infants, need larger amount of zinc (per kg body weight) for their development and growth and so they are liable to zinc deficiency. In fact, the minimum zinc concentration as low as 10.7 ppm corresponding to about 1/12 of the control level was observed in a 2-year-old boy (Fig. 2), and the lowest mean concentration level was observed in the infant group aged 0–3 years-old in both sexes (male: 87 ppm; female: 81 ppm) (Table 1). These findings indicate that a considerable number of autistic children, in particular infants, are suffered from marginal to severe zinc deficiency, suggesting that infantile zinc deficiency may play a role in the neural development disorders and pathogenesis of autism spectrum disorders, and zinc supplementation may be useful for treatment and prevention of some patients with autistic disorders and suspects.

The incidence rate of zinc deficiency in the age group of 4–9 and 10–15 years-old was estimated 28.1 and 3.3 % in male, and 28.7 and 3.5 % in female subjects, respectively, indicating that there is little gender difference in zinc deficiency rate in the autistic subjects. It remains to be explained why the elder subjects over 10-year-old have normal zinc concentration, although this is maybe explained by the possibility that the young adolescents have better metal-protein functioning and utilize dietary zinc more efficiently and effectively. There were some studies reporting lower serum zinc levels in children with attention deficit hyperactivity disorder (ADHD) in developing countries[24,31]. Recently, zinc deficiency has been remarked in not only developing but also developed countries, due to imbalanced intake of trace nutrients and dieting[32,33]. Faber et al.[34] reported that the mean plasma Zn/Cu ratio in children with autistic disorder was below the cut-off value of the lowest 2.5 % of healthy children, suggesting that plasma zinc/copper ratio may be a bio-marker of heavy metal toxicity in children with autism spectrum disorders. Other clinical studies reported that mean serum zinc levels were significantly lower in both autism and ADHD groups, and that serum zinc level correlated inversely with parent- and teacher-rated inattention in ADHD children[33]. Furthermore, zinc treatment was reported significantly superior to placebo in reducing symptoms of hyperactivity, impulsivity and impaired socialization in ADHD patients[35,36]. The other human study showed that many children with ADHD have lower zinc concentration in comparison to healthy children, and zinc supplement as an adjunct to methylphenidate has favorable effects in the treatment of ADHD children, pointing to the possible association of zinc deficiency and ADHD pathophysiology[37].The cellular zinc homeostasis is mediated by two transporter families: the zinc-importer (Zip) family that transport zinc into the cytosol, and the zinc transporter (ZnT) family transporting zinc out of the cytosol[38]. The severe zinc deficiency in a rare inherited human disease ''acrodermatitis enteropathy'' is reported to result from defective intestinal absorption of zinc by mutations in the Zip4 transporter located on intestinal duct[39,40]. Autistic children have often been reported to have gastrointestinal problems of intestinal malabsorption of nutrients[41], named ''leaky gut syndrome'' which may lead to zinc deficiency, and zinc deficiency itself may further lead to gut syndrome resulting from over-consumption of fructose[42]. Furthermore, many of the autistic children are also suffered from allergic disorders that are known to relate to zinc deficiency. Thus, these findings suggest that infantile zinc deficiency may be also responsible for the pathogenesis of various allergic symptoms observed in the children with autistic spectrum disorders.

Recently, dietary restriction-induced zinc deficiency has been reported to up-regulate intestinal zinc-importer (Zip4) and induce the increase in Zip4 protein located to the plasma membrane of enterocytes[43]. This adoptive response to zinc deficiency is known to lead to increasing in the risk of high-uptake of toxic metals such as cadmium and lead. Thus, infants with zinc deficiency are liable to be exposed to increased risk of absorbing high amounts of toxic metals and retaining them in their body. These findings suggest that increased risk of toxic metal burdens attendant on the infantile zinc deficiency may also contribute to the pathogenesis of autistic spectrum disorders.

The mechanisms of zinc deficiency in autistic infants and ADHD children may be explained by their unbalanced nutritional intake and lower absorption ability in intestinal duct[41,44]. In addition, maternal cigarette smoking has been reported to be associated with lower zinc and higher cadmium and lead concentrations in their neonates[45]. Because of their high distribution property to bone tissue, during pregnancy and lactation, these toxic metals accumulated in the maternal bone matrix are co-transferred with calcium and magnesium to fetal and newborn bodies through increased bone-resorption[45–47].

Kern et al. [48] reported that arsenic, cadmium and lead were significantly lower in the hair of children with autism than in matched controls, and the patients have trouble excreting these toxic elements. We also reported that not only toxic but also some essential metals are significantly lower in autistic children[13], suggesting that the patients with zinc deficiency have a low excretion ability of toxic metals and result in a higher body burden with them.

Eklund and Oskarsson[49] reported that soy-based formulas contain approxi mate six times more cadmium than cow's milk formulas, and cereal-based formulas have 4–21 times higher levels. Thus, the dietary intake of cadmium may be higher in the children feeding on infant formulas and weaning foods, compared to breast milk-fed infants.

In conclusion, this preliminary study shows that many of infants with autistic spectrum disorders have been suffered from marginal to severe zinc deficiency. This finding suggests that infantile zinc deficiency and attendant toxic metal accumulation may play principal roles in the pathogenesis of autism, in particular, through their epigenetic modifications. Furthermore, these findings suggest the possibility that some of autistic children and suspects may be improved by nutritional approach supplementing deficient nutrients such as zinc, on the basis of evidence data, although zinc supplementation should be applied for infantile patients rather than elder group over 10-year-old. This evidence-based nutritional approach may yield a novel pathway into prevention and treatment of the children with autism spectrum disorders in near future. Controlled studies for this nutritional approach are desirable to establish the principal roles of infantile zinc deficiency and toxic metal burdens in the neural development disorders and pathogenesis of autism.

Methods

Sampling and zinc analysis. On the basis of informed consent, scalp hair samples from 1,967 (male: 1,553; female: 414) subjects aged 0–15 years were collected in the period from June 2005 to September 2007, although 0 year-old subject was only one (11 month-old female). These subjects were comprised of the children diagnosed with autistic spectrum disorders by their physicians. Hair sampling was recommended to cut as close to the scalp of the occipital area as possible.

Hair sample of 75 mg was weighed into 50ml plastic tube, and washed with acetone and then with 0.01% Triton solution, in accordance with the procedures recommended by the Hair Analysis Standardization Board. The washed hair sample was mixed with 10 ml 6.25% tetra methyl ammonium hydroxide (TMAH, Tama Chemical, Kawasaki, Japan) and 50 micro-L 0.1% gold solution (SPEX Certi Prep, Metuchen, NJ, USA), and then dissolved at 75 degrees C with shaking for 2 hours. After cooling the solution to room temperature, internal standard solution was added, and after adjusting its volume gravimetric, the obtained solution was used for zinc analysis. The zinc concentrations were determined with inductively coupled plasma mass spectrometry (ICP-MS; 7500ce, Agilent Technologies, Santa Clara, CA, USA) by the internal standard method and expressed as ng/g hair (ppb) or micro-g/g (ppm) [17,18]. The method detection limit for zinc determination was 12 ng/g hair (ppb), and human hair certified reference material (NIES CRM No. 13) was used to check for the accuracy of analysis. The inter-daily variation of zinc determination was calculated 2.2 %. The control zinc reference range of 86.3–193 ppm, its geometric mean ±2 S.D. level, obtained from the data for healthy 436 male subjects aged 21-40 years-old was close to that for healthy female adults, as previously reported[17,18,50], furthermore almost consisting with those reported by the other research groups[10-12]. This control zinc reference range was also almost consistent with those for nutritionally controlled children[13] and for the Vancouver preschoolers aged 2-5 years-old (N = 719)[28], but somewhat different from the age-matched reference data for neurotypical control children in which the 11 % participants had been medicated as reviewed by Adams[30].

This study has been approved by review of the ethical committee of La Belle Vie research laboratory. All of the data obtained are held securely in such a form as to ensure anonymity.

Statistical analysis. Because scalp hair mineral concentration is log-normally distributed, the zinc concentration was converted to logarithm, and the geometric rather than arithmetic mean was used as representative of its hair concentration. The relation between age and zinc concentrations of the subjects was examined by Pearson's correlation coefficient test.

References

1. Pinto, D. *et al.* Functional impact of global rare copy number variation in autism spectrum disorders. *Nature* 466, 368–372 (2010).
2. Chakrabarti, S. & Fombonne, E. Pervasive developmental disorders in preschool children: confirmation of high prevalence. *Am. J. Psychiatry* 162, 1133–1141 (2005).
3. Bailey, A. *et al.* Autism as a strongly genetic disorder: evidence from a British twin study. *Psychol. Med.* 25, 63–77 (1995).
4. Marshall, C. R. *et al.* Structural variation of chromosomes in autism spectrum disorder. *Am. J. Hum. Genet.* 82, 477–488 (2008).
5. Dufault, R. *et al.* Mercury exposure, nutritional deficiencies and metabolic disruptions may affect learning in children. *Behav. Brain Funct.* 5, 44–58 (2009).
6. O'Rahilly, S. Human genetics illuminates the paths to metabolic disease. *Nature* 462, 307–314 (2009).
7. Jin, Y. H. *et al.* Cadmium is a mutagen that acts by inhibiting mismatch repair. *Nat. Genet.* 34, 239–241 (2003).

8. Takiguchi, M., Achanzar, W. E., Qu, W., Li, G. & Waalkes, M. P. Effects of cadmium on DNA-(cytosine-5) methyltransferase activity and DNA methylation status during cadmium-induced cellular transformation. *Exp. Cell Res.* 286, 355–365 (2003).

9. Arita, A. & Costa, M. Epigenetics in metal carcinogenesis: nickel, arsenic, chromium and cadmium. *Metallomics* 1, 222–228 (2009).

10. Rodushkin, I. & Axelsson, M. D. Application of double focusing sector field ICP-MS for multi elemental characterization of human hair and nails. Part 1. Analytical methodology. *Sci. Total Environ.* 250, 83–100 (2000).

11. Goulle, J. P. *et al.* Metal and metalloid multi-elementary ICP-MS validation in whole blood, plasma, urine and hair: Reference values. *Forens. Sci. Intern.* 153, 39– 44 (2005).

12. Wang, C. T., Chang, W. T., Zeng, W. F. & Lin, C. H. Concentrations of calcium, copper, iron, magnesium, potassium, sodium and zinc in adult female hair with different body mass indexes in Taiwan. *Clin. Chem. Lab. Med.* 43, 389–393 (2005).

13. Munakata, M. *et al.* A preliminary analysis of trace elements in the scalp hair of patients with severe motor disabilities receiving enteral nutrition. *Brain Development* 28, 521–525 (2006).

14. Yasuda, H., Yonashiro, T., Yoshida, K., Ishii, T. & Tsutsui, T. Mineral imbalance in children with autistic disorders. *Biomed. Res. Trace Elem.* 16, 285–291 (2005).

15. Adams, J. B., Holloway, C. E., George, F. & Quig, D. Analyses of toxic metals and essential minerals in the hair of Arizona children with autism and associated conditions, and their mothers. *Biol. Trace Elem. Res.* 110, 193–209 (2006).

16. Adams, J. B. *et al.* The severity of autism is associated with toxic metal body burden and red blood cell glutathione levels. *J. Toxicol.* 2009, 532640 (2009).

17. Yasuda, H., Yonashiro, T., Yoshida, K., Ishii, T. & Tsutsui, T. Relationship between body mass index and minerals in male Japanese adults. *Biomed. Res. Trace Elem.* 17, 316–321 (2006).

18. Yasuda, H. *et al.* Metallomics study using hair mineral analysis and multiple logistic regression analysis: relationship between cancer and minerals. *Environ. Health Prev. Med.* 14, 261–266 (2009).

19. Pilch, S. M. & Senti, F. R. Analysis of zinc data from the second national health and nutrition examination survey (NHANES II). *J. Nutr.* 115, 1393–1397 (1985).

20. Yasuda, H., Yonashiro, T., Yoshida, K., Ishii, T. & Tsutsui, T. High toxic

metal levels in scalp hair of infants and children. *Biomed. Res. Trace Elem.* 16, 39–45 (2005).

21. Yasuda, H., Yoshida, K., Segawa, M., Tokuda, R., Yasuda, Y. & Tsutsui, T. High accumulation of aluminium in hairs of infants and children. *Biomed. Res. Trace Elem.* 19, 57–62 (2008).

22. Yasuda, H., Yoshida, K., Yasuda, Y. & Tsutsui, T. Two age-related accumulation profiles of toxic metals. *Cur. Aging Sci.* 4, (2011) (in press) PMID: 21834789.

23. Prasad, A. S. Impact of the discovery of human zinc deficiency on health. *J. Am. Coll. Nutr.* 28, 257–265 (2009).

24. DiGirolamo, A. M. & Raminez-Zea, M. Role of zinc in maternal and child mental health. *Am. J. Clin. Nutr.* 89(suppl), 940S–945S (2009).

25. Gibson, R. S., Vanderkooy, P. D., MacDonald, A. C., Goldman, A., Ryan, B. A. & Berry, M. A. Growth-limiting, mild zinc-deficiency syndrome in some southern Ontario boys with low height percentiles. *Am. J. Clin. Nutr.* 49, 1266–1273 (1989).

26. Walravens, P. A., Krebs, N. F. & Hambidge, K. M. Linear growth of low income preschool children receiving a zinc supplement. *Am. J. Clin. Nutr.* 38, 195–201 (1983).

27. Gibson, R. S. Assessment of trace element status in humans. *Prog. Food Nutr. Sci.* 13, 67–111 (1989).

28. Vaghri, Z., Barr, S., Wong, H., Chapman, G. & Hertzman, C. Age-based differences in hair zinc of Vancouver preschoolers. *Biol. Trace Elem. Res.* 126, S21–S30 (2008).

29. Vaghri, Z., Wong, H., Barr, S., Chapman, G. & Hertzman, C. Associations of socio-demographic and behavioural variables with hair zinc of Vancouver preschoolers. *Biol. Trace Elem. Res.* 129, (2011) PMID: 21369714.

30. Adams, J. B. *et al.* Nutritional and metabolic status of children with autism vs. neurotypical children, and the association with autism severity. *Nutr. Metab.* 8, 34–65 (2011).

31. Arnold, L. E. & DiSilvestro, R. A. Zinc in attention-deficit/hyperactivity disorder. *J. Child Adolesc. Psychopharmacol.* 15, 619–627 (2005).

32. Plum, L. M., Rink, L. & Haase, H. The essential toxin: Impact of zinc on human health. *Int. J. Environ. Res. Public Health* 7, 1342–1365 (2010).

33. Arnold, L. E. *et al.* Serum zinc correlates with parent- and teacher-rated inattention in children with attention-deficit/hyperactivity disorder. *J. Child Adolesc. Psychopharmacol.* 15, 628–636 (2005).

34. Faber, S., Zinn, G. M., Faber, S., Zinn, G. M., Kern, J. C. & Kingston, H. M.

The plasma zinc/serum copper ratio as a biomarker in children with autism spectrum disorders. *Biomarkers* 14, 171–180 (2009).
35. Yorbik, O., Ozdag, M. F., Olgun, A., Senol, M. G., Bek, S. & Akman, S. Potential effects of zinc on information processing in boys with attention deficit hyper- activity disorder. *Prog. Neuropsychopharmacol. Biol. Psychiatry* 32, 662–667 (2008).
36. DiGirolamo, A. M. *et al.* Randomized trial of the effect of zinc supplementation on the mental health of school-age children in Guatemala. *Am. J. Clin. Nutr.* 92, 1241–1250 (2010).
37. Akhondzadeh, S., Mohammadi, M. R. & Khademi, M. Zinc sulfate as an adjunct to methylphenidate for the treatment of attention deficit hyperactivity disorder in children: a double blind and randomised trial [ISRCTN64132371]. *B.M.C. Psychiatry* 4, 9–14 (2004).
38. Lichten, L. A. & Cousins, R. J. Mammalian zinc transporters: nutritional and physiologic regulation. *Ann. Rev. Nutr.* 29, 153–176 (2009).
39. Wang, K., Zhou, B., Kuo, Y., Zemansky, J. & Gitschier, J. A novel member of a zinc transporter family is defective in acrodermatitis enteropathica. *Am. J. Hum. Genet.* 71, 66–73 (2002).
40. Dufner-Beattie, J., Wang, F., Kuo, Y. M., Gitschier, J., Eide, D. & Andrews, G. K. The acrodermatitis enteropathica gene ZIP4 encodes a tissue-specific, zinc- regulated zinc transporter in mice. *J. Biol. Chem.* 278, 33474–33481 (2003).
41. Adams, J. B., Johansen, L. J., Powell, L. D., Quig, D. & Rubin, R. A. Gastrointestinal flora and gastrointestinal status in children with autism – comparisons to typical children and correlation with autism severity. *BMC Gastroenterology* 11, 22–34 (2011).
42. Lustig, R. H. Fructose: metabolic, hedonic, and social parallels with ethanol. *J. Am. Diet. Assoc.* 110, 1307–1321 (2010).
43. Cousins, R. J., Liuzzi, J. P. & Lichten, L. A. Mammalian zinc transport, trafficking, and signals. *J. Biol. Chem.* 281, 24085–24089 (2006).
44. Dodig-Curkovic, K., Dovhanj, J., Curkovic´, M., Dodig-Radic´, J. & Degmecic´, D. The role of zinc in the treatment of hyperactivity disorder in children. *Acta Med. Croatica* 63, 307–313 (2009).
45. Razagui, I. B. & Ghribi, I. Maternal and neonatal scalp hair concentrations of zinc, cadmium, and lead: relationship to some lifestyle factors. *Biol. Trace Elem. Res.* 106, 1–28 (2005).
46. Symanski, E. & Hertz-Picciotto, I. Blood lead levels in relation to menopause, smoking, and pregnancy history. *Am. J. Epidemiol.* 141, 1047–1058

(1995).

47. Gulson, B. L., Jameson, C. W., Mahaffey, K. R., Mizon, K. J., Korsch, M. J. & Vimpani, G. Pregnancy increases mobilization of lead from maternal skeleton. *J. Lab. Clin. Med.* 130, 51–62 (1997).

48. Kern, J. K., Granneman, B. D., Trivedi, M. H. & Adams, J. B. Sulfhydryl-reactive metals in autism. *J. Toxicol. Environm. Health* 70, 715–721 (2007).

49. Eklund, G. & Oskarsson, A. Exposure of cadmium from infant formulas and weaning foods. *Food Addit. Contam.* 16, 509–519 (1999).

50. Yasuda, H., Yoshida, K., Fukuchi, K., Tokuda, R., Tsutsui, T. & Yonei, Y. Association of aging with minerals in Japanese male adults. *Anti-Aging Med.* 4, 38–42 (2007).

Chapter 2:

ESTIMATION OF AUTISTIC CHILDREN BY METALLOMICS ANALYSIS

(Comprehensive Mineral Analysis)

published in **Scientific Reports 3: 129 (2013).**

Hiroshi Yasuda[1], Yuichi Yasuda[2] & Toyoharu Tsutsui[1]
[1]La Belle Vie Research Laboratory, Chuo-ku, Tokyo; [2]Health Science Laboratory, Tokyo, Japan.

Abstract: Clarification of the pathogenesis and treatment of autism spectrum disorders is one of the challenges today. In this study, we examine scalp hair concentrations of 26 trace elements for 1,967 children with autistic disorders (1,553 males and 414 females). Five-hundred and eighty-four (29.7%), 347 (17.6%) and 114 (5.8%) subjects was found deficient in zinc, magnesium and calcium, respectively, and 2.0% or less in the other essential metals. The incidence rate of mineral deficiency was highly observed in infants aged 0-3 years-old. In contrast, 339 (17.2%), 168 (8.5%) and 94 (4.8%) individuals was found suffering from high burden of aluminium, cadmium and lead, and 2.8% or less from mercury and arsenic burden. These findings suggest that infantile zinc- and magnesium-deficiency and/or toxic metal burdens may epigenetically play principal roles as environmental factors in autistic disorders and that metallomics approach may lead to early screening and prevention of the neurodevelopment disorders.

Autism spectrum disorders are a group of neural development disorders characterized by impairments in social interaction and communication, and by the presence of restricted and repetitive behaviours[1,2], and the prevalence of this disease continues to increase up to 1 in 88 children[1–4]. Autism spectrum disorders are known to be highly heritable and some related genes have been reported[5,6]. However, the critical genetic determinants are still unclarified[2,4], and the interaction of heritable factors with uncertified lifestyle and environmental factors seem play a significant role in the etiology. For example, organic mercury had been claimed one of environmental candidates causing autistic disorders[7], but its relationship remains to be established. Recently, epigenetic alteration of gene expression by environmental factors is considered one of key events in the pathogenesis of genetic diseases[8], and some toxic elements such as cadmium and arsenic have been reported to be candidate factors that induce epigenetic disorders[9–13].

Recent great advances in high-sensitive and reliable trace element analysis method using inductively coupled plasma mass spectrometry (ICP-MS) have enabled us to apply it to forensic medical researches and estimating chronic toxic metal burden and mineral deficiency in human body[14,15]. Thus, clinical applications of the reliable hair mineral analysis method with ICP-MS have been tried for investigating the association of some diseases and symptoms with trace element kinetics including toxic metals and essential minerals[16–21].

For the last six years, we have examined the association of toxic metal burdens with autistic disorders and reported that some of the autistic children have suffered from high accumulation of toxic metals such as cadmium, lead or aluminium[22–24]. Recently, we demonstrated the association of infantile zinc deficiency with autism spectrum disorders[25].

In this metallomics analysis study, we have determined human scalp hair concentrations of 26 trace elements for 1,967 children with autistic disorders aged 0–15 years and showed that many of the patients, especially in infants aged 0–3 years-old, are suffering from marginal to severe zinc- and magnesium-deficiency and/or high burdens of several toxic metals such as aluminium, cadmium and lead. These findings suggest that there is a critical term ''infantile window'' in neurodevelopment and probable for therapy of autistic disorders.

Results

The histogram of hair logarithmic zinc concentrations for 1,967 children with autistic spectrum disorders is shown in Figure 1. The distribution of the zinc concentration was non-symmetric with tailing in lower range, and 584 in 1,967 subjects (29.7%) were found to have lower zinc concentration than –2 S.D. (standard deviation) level of the reference range (86.3–193 ppm; geometric mean = 129 ppm), estimated as zinc deficiency. The incidence rate of zinc deficiency in the age groups of 0–3, 4–9 and 10–15 years-old was estimated 43.5, 28.1 and 3.3% in male and 52.5, 28.7 and 3.5% in female, respectively (Table 1), and a significant correlation of zinc concentration with age ($r = 0.367$, $p < 0.0001$) was observed (Fig. 2), indicating that infants are more liable to zinc deficiency than elder children. The minimum zinc concentration of 10.7 ppm detected in a 2-year-old boy corresponded to about 1/12 of the mean reference level. The zinc concentration of only one 0 year-old female subject was 173 ppm in the normal range (Fig. 2) and seem be a suspect, because she was suffered from high burdens of aluminium (52.5 ppm), lead (9.1 ppm), iron (12.8 ppm) and copper (134 ppm). There was no significant gender difference in hair zinc concentration and incidence rate of zinc deficiency.

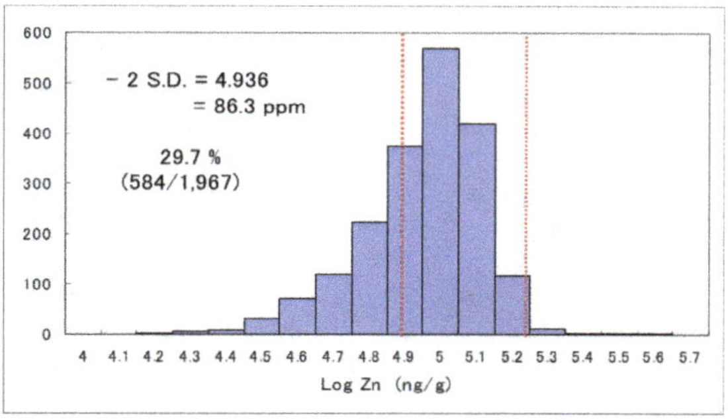

Figure 1 | Histogram of logarithmic zinc concentration in autistic children.

The histogram of scalp hair zinc concentrations for 1,967 children (1,553 males and 414 females) aged 0–15 years is shown in the logarithm. The numbers on the abscissa indicate the logarithm of scalp hair zinc concentration (ng/g: ppb). The height of each rectangle represents the frequency in the class interval in logarithmic hair zinc level. Two dotted vertical lines represent the ±2 S.D. levels of the reference range of hair zinc concentrations.

Table 1 | Incidence rate of zinc deficiency and the minimum level in autistic children

The number and incidence rate of individuals with zinc deficiency (lower than -2 S.D.) in 1,967 autistic children (1,553 males and 414 females) and the minimum zinc concentration in each age group are tabled

	Age	No.	Number of Cases with Zn Deficiency	Rate (%) of Zn Deficiency	Minimum (ppm)
Male	0–3 year-old	577	251	43.5	10.7
	4–9 year-old	736	207	28.1	21.3
	10–15year-old	240	8	3.3	66.1
Female	0–3 year-old	118	62	52.5	17.3
	4–9 year-old	181	52	28.7	35.7
	10–15 ear-old	115	4	3.5	72.4

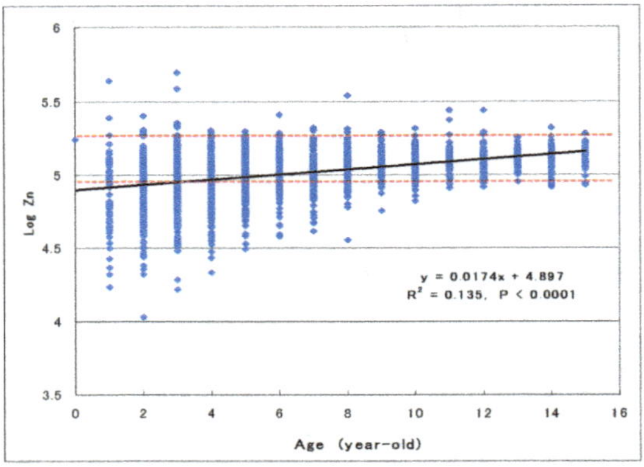

Figure 2 | Relation of logarithmic zinc concentration with age in autistic children

The association of hair logarithmic zinc concentration with age in autistic children (N = 1,967) is shown. Each point represents the corresponding age and logarithmic zinc concentration of the individual child. Two dotted horizontal lines represent the ±2 S.D. levels of the reference range (86.3-193 ppm) of zinc concentration. Significant relation of the zinc concentration with age ($r = 0.367$, $p < 0.0001$) in the autistic children is shown.

Following to zinc deficiency, magnesium and calcium deficiency was observed in 347 (17.6%) and 114 (5.8%) individuals in the autistic children (Table 2), and for the other essential metals such as iron, chromium, manganese, copper and cobalt, their incidence rates of deficiency were 2.0% or less.

Table 2 | Incidence rate of mineral deficiency in autistic children. The number and incidence rate of individuals with mineral deficiency (lower than -2 S.D.) in 1,967 autistic children (1,553 males and 414 females) are tabled.

Mineral	Number of Cases with Deficiency	Rate (%) of Deficiency
Zn	584	29.7
Mg	347	17.6
Ca	114	5.8
Co	40	2.0
Fe	17	0.9
Cr	12	0.6
Mn	4	0.2
Cu	4	0.2

The incidence rate of magnesium deficiency in the age groups of 0–3, 4–9 and 10–15 years-old was 27.0, 17.1 and 4.2% in male and 22.9, 12.7 and 4.3% in female subjects, respectively (Table 3), and a significant correlation of magnesium concentration with age ($r = 0.362$, $p < 0.0001$) was observed (Fig. 3), suggesting that infants are also liable to magnesium deficiency than elder children. The minimal magnesium concentration of 3.88 ppm detected in a 2-year-old girl corresponded to almost 1/10 of the mean reference level (39.5 ppm). Calcium deficiency was observed only in lower age groups less than 10 years-old (Table 4).

Table 3 | Incidence rate of magnesium deficiency and the minimum level in autistic children.
The number and incidence rate of individuals with magnesium deficiency (lower than -2 S.D.) in 1,967 autistic children (1,553 males and 414 females) and the minimum magnesium concentration in each age group are table.

	Age	Number of Cases with Mg Deficiency	Rate (%) of Mg Deficiency	Minimum (ppm)
Male	0–3 year–old	156	27.0	3.92
	4–9 year–old	126	17.1	4.19
	10–15 year–old	10	4.2	5.31
Female	0–3 year–old	27	22.9	3.88
	4–9 year–old	23	12.7	4.75
	10–15 year–old	5	4.3	6.27

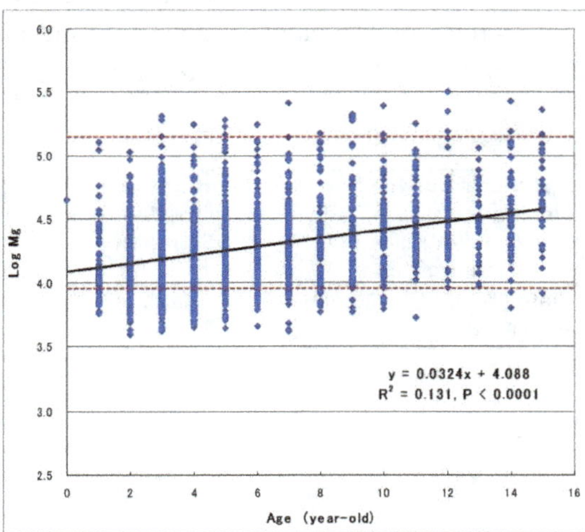

Figure 3 | Relation of logarithmic magnesium concentration with age in autistic children. The association of hair logarithmic magnesium concentration with age in autistic children (N =1,967) is shown. Each point represents the corresponding age and logarithmic magnesium concentration of the individual child. The dotted horizontal lines represent the ±2 S.D. levels of the reference range (9.6–163 ppm) of hair magnesium concentrations. A significant relation of the magnesium concentration with age ($r = 0.362$, $p < 0.0001$) in the autistic children is shown.

In contrast, high toxic metal burden of aluminium, cadmium and lead of over their +2 S.D. level was observed in 339 (17.2%), 168 (8.5%) and 94

(4.8%) individuals, and their incidence rates were higher than that of mercury and arsenic (2.8 and 2.6%, respectively) (Table 5). The detected maximal

Table 4 | Incidence rate of calcium deficiency and the minimum level in autistic children. The number and incidence rate of individuals with calcium deficiency (lower than -2 S.D.) in 1,967 autistic children (1,553 males and 414 females) and the minimum calcium concentration in each age group are tabled.

	Age	Number of Cases with Ca Deficiency	Rate (%) of Ca Deficiency	Minimum (ppm)
Male	0–3 year–old	60	10.4	70.1
	4–9 year–old	45	6.1	67.5
	10–15 year–old	1	0.4	95.5
Female	0–3 year–old	4	3.4	88.2
	4–9 year–old	3	1.7	95.4
	10–15 year–old	1	0.9	90.2

concentration of aluminium, cadmium and lead was 79.4 ppm in a 4-year-old boy, 5.47 ppm in a 5-year-old boy and 24.9 ppm in a 5-year-old girl, respectively, corresponding to 21-, 782- and 57-fold of each mean reference level. The maximal burden level of mercury and arsenic was 36.3 ppm and 1.7 ppm, respectively, corresponding to about 9- and 33-fold of the mean reference level.

Table 5 | Incidence rate of high toxic metal burden and the maximum level in autistic children. The number and incidence rate of individuals with high toxic metal burden (higher than +2 S.D.) in 1,967 autistic children (1,553 males and 414 females) and the maximum concentration are tabled.

Toxic Metal	Number of Cases with High Burden	Rate (%) of High Burden	Maximum (ppm)	Ratio to Reference
Al	339	17.2	79.4	21.1
Cd	168	8.5	5.5	782.0
Pb	94	4.8	24.9	57.4
Hg	56	2.8	36.3	9.3
As	52	2.6	1.7	33.5

Figure 4 shows a typical autistic metallome profile in a 1-year-old boy suffering from severe zinc- and magnesium-deficiency and simultaneous high burdens of cadmium and lead. Another autistic metallome profile with high burdens of aluminium and manganese in a 2-year-old boy is shown in Figure 5.

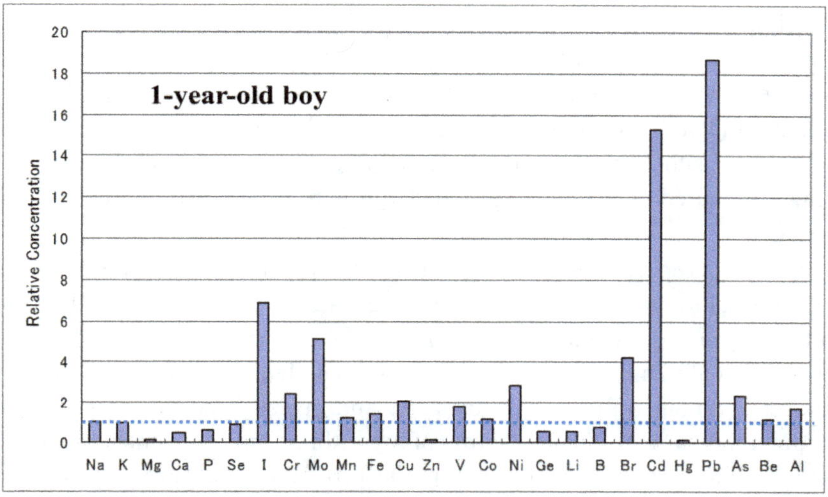

Figure 4 | Metallome profile of an autistic child with high cadmium and lead burdens. A typical metallome profile of 1-year-old boy diagnosed with autism is shown, exhibiting severe zinc- and magnesium-deficiency and simultaneous high burdens with cadmium (107 ppb) and lead (8.11 ppm). Each bar represents the relative concentration of the respective trace element in his scalp hair specimen. The dotted horizontal line at 1.0 represents the reference control level of each trace element disorders and that there is a critical term "infantile window" in neurodevelopment and for its therapy.

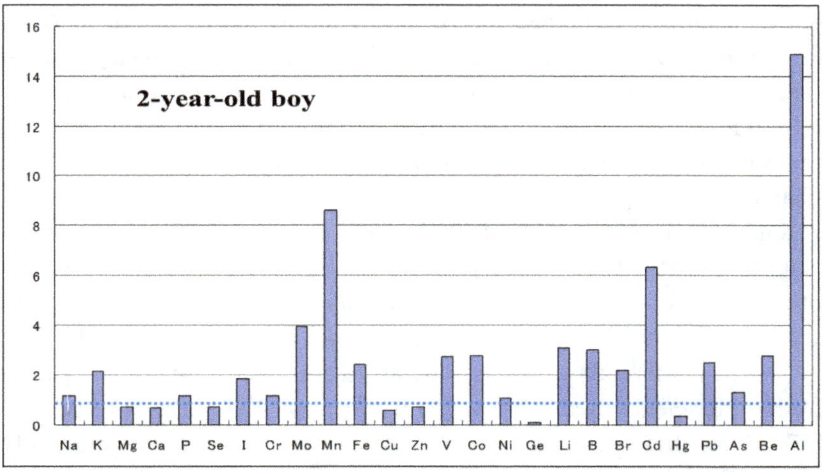

Figure 5 | Metallome profile of an autistic child with high aluminium and manganese burdens. Another typical metallome profile of 2-year-old boy diagnosed with autism is shown, exhibiting simultaneous high burdens with aluminium (55.9 ppm), manganese (926 ppb) and cadmium (44 ppb). Each bar represents the relative concentration of the respective trace element in his hair specimen. The dotted horizontal line at 1.0 represents the reference control level of each trace element.

Discussion

Zinc is an essential trace element that plays important roles in nucleic acid/protein synthesis, cell replication, tissue growth and repair, especially in pregnant women and infants. Therefore, zinc deficiency is known associated with various pathological conditions, including dysgeusia, delayed wound healing, impaired immunity, retarded growth, and neural-degenerative diseases[26–30].

Recently we reported that many infants with autistic disorders are suffered from marginal to severe zinc deficiency, suggesting considerable relationship of infantile zinc deficiency with autism[25]. In the present study, we have determined scalp hair concentrations of 26 trace elements for 1,967 subjects diagnosed with autism spectrum disorders and investigated their association with mineral disorders. The histogram of logarithmic zinc concentration in the autistic children showed a non-symmetric profile with a marked tailing in lower range, indicating that about 30% of the autistic children were estimated as zinc deficiency (Fig. 1). In particular, nearly one half (male: 43.5%; female: 52.5%) of the infant group aged 0–3 year-old were found to suffer from marginal to severe zinc deficiency (Table 1). Thus, the lowest mean zinc concentration was observed in the infant group aged 0–3 years-old in both genders (male: 87 ppm; female: 81 ppm), and a high significant correlation of the zinc concentration with age was observed in the autistic children (Fig. 2). These findings suggest that infants are liable to zinc deficiency because they need larger amount of zinc (per kg body weight) for their development and growth. In addition, age-related changes in the production of metallothionein proteins and differences in glutathione levels may be associated with the age-related differences in zinc requirements[31]. There was little gender difference in zinc deficiency rate and also in hair zinc concentration (Table 1).

Next to zinc deficiency, a considerable number of autistic children were found to be deficient in magnesium and calcium, and no significant deficiency was observed for the other essential metals (Table 2). The incidence rate of magnesium deficiency in the age group of 0–3 and 4–9 years-old was 27.0 and 17.1% in male, and 22.9 and 12.7% in female subjects, respectively, suggesting that about one fourth of the infant group are suffered from a simultaneous deficiency of zinc and magnesium. Compared to magnesium, significant deficiency in calcium was observed only in the lower age groups (Table 4). These findings indicate that infantile autistic children have a character liable to deficiency in zinc and magnesium.

There are numerous studies with the same theme reporting nutritional status and mineral deficiencies in autistic children[32–36]. However, the conclusions of their studies, in which the restricted subject age range (over 3 or 5 years-old) and number of minerals were examined, were not consistent, and the critical environmental factors remained to be established. In this metallomics analysis study for the 1,967 autistic children aged 0–15 years-old, we were able to demonstrate not only the critical epigenetic factor (zinc- and magnesium-deficiency and/or high burdens of aluminium, cadmium and lead) but also the presence of another critical factor, ''infantile window'' in neurodevelopment and for therapy probably.

Arnold et al.[37] reported that mean serum zinc levels were significantly lower in both autism and ADHD groups, and that serum zinc level correlated inversely with parent- and teacher-rated inattention in ADHD children. Furthermore, it is reported that zinc treatment was significantly superior to placebo in reducing symptoms of hyperactivity, impulsivity and impaired socialization in ADHD patients[38,39]. Other preliminary human study showed that many children with ADHD have lower zinc concentration in comparison to healthy children and that zinc supplement as an adjunct to methylphenidate has favorable effects in the treatment of ADHD children, pointing to the possible association of zinc deficiency and ADHD pathophysiology[40].

Kozielec et al.[41] have reported that in hyperactive 116 children with ADHD, magnesium deficiency was found in the 95% of the subjects, most frequently in hair (77.6%), next in red-blood cells (58.6%) and in blood serum (33.6%). Furthermore, they reported that a significant decrease of hyperactivity and increase in hair magnesium contents has been achieved in the group of ADHD children given six months of magnesium supplementation[42]. Mousain-Bosc et al.[43] also reported that 52 hyper-excitable children have low intra-erythrocyte magnesium levels with normal serum magnesium values and that magnesium/vitamin B6 supplementation can restore the erythrocyte magnesium levels to normal and improve their abnormal behaviors. They also reported that thirty-three children with clinical symptoms of pervasive developmental disorder (PDD) or autism exhibit significantly lower red blood cell magnesium values and that the combination therapy with magnesium/vitamin B6 for six months improved significantly PDD symptoms in 23/33 children ($p < 0.0001$) with concomitant increases in intra-erythrocyte magnesium values[44].

These findings are consistent with a gradient overarching disorder hypothesis for autism spectrum disorders and ADHD[45] and indicate that infantile mineral deficiency in zinc and magnesium plays epigenetically principal roles as environmental factors in the pathogenesis of these neurodevelopment disorders, suggesting that the supplementation of deficient minerals during the critical ''infantile window'' may be useful for treatment and prevention of these diseases.

Recently, dietary restriction-induced zinc deficiency has been reported to up-regulate intestinal zinc-importer (ZIP4) and induce the increase in ZIP4 protein located to the plasma membrane of enterocytes[46,47]. This adoptive response to zinc deficiency is known to lead to increase in the risk of high-uptake of toxic metals such as cadmium and lead[48]. Thus, infants with zinc deficiency are liable to increased risk of absorbing high amount of toxic metals and retaining them in their bodies, as shown in Table 5 and Fig. 4. These findings suggest that the increased toxic metal burdens attendant on zinc deficiency may also epigenetically contribute to the pathogenesis of these diseases.

Maternal cigarette smoking has been reported to be associated with lower zinc and higher cadmium and lead concentrations in their neonates[49]. During pregnancy and lactation, these toxic metals accumulated in the maternal bone tissues are co-transferred with calcium to fetal and new-born bodies through activated bone-resorption[49–52].

Eklund and Oskarsson[53] reported that soy-based formulas contain approximately six times more cadmium than cow's milk formulas and cereal-based formulas have 4–21 times higher levels. Thus, the dietary intake of the toxic metal in the children fed on infant formulas and weaning foods may be high in comparison with breast milk-fed infants.

For mercury and arsenic, the maximum burden level of 9.3- and 33.5-fold of the reference level (Table 5) may also epigenetically play some pathogenic roles in the respective autistic individuals, even though their incidence rate was 2.8% or less.

In summary, this metallomics study demonstrates that many of autistic infants have been suffered from marginal to severe zinc- and magnesium-deficiency and/or high toxic metal burdens of aluminium, cadmium, lead and so on. These findings suggest that infantile mineral deficiency and/or toxic metal burdens may epigenetically play principal roles in the pathogenesis of autism spectrum disorders and that there is a critical "infantile window" in neurodevelopment and for its therapy. Therefore, it is possible that autistic infants may respond to nutritional approach supplementing deficient nutrients and detoxifying accumulated toxic metals on the basis of the evidence. This evidence-based nutritional approach may yield a new pathway into treatment and prevention of infantile patients with autistic disorders including the suspects. Well-controlled intervention studies for this novel nutritional therapy are desired to establish the epigenetic roles of infantile mineral deficiencies and/or toxic metal burdens in the pathogenesis of neurodevelopment disorders such as autism spectrum disorders and ADHD.

In conclusion, this preliminary study demonstrates that many of infantile patients diagnosed with autism have been suffered from marginal to severe zinc- and magnesium-deficiency and/or high toxic metal burdens of aluminium, cadmium, lead and so on, suggesting that these mineral disorders may epigenetically play principal roles as environmental factors in the pathogenesis of neurodevelopment disorders.

Methods

Samples and trace element analysis. On the basis of informed consent, scalp hair samples from 1,967 (male: 1,553; female: 414) autistic Japanese subjects aged 0–15 years were collected in the period from June 2005 to September 2007, although 0 year-old subject was only one (11 month-old female). These subjects were comprised of the children diagnosed with autistic spectrum disorders by their physicians. Hair sampling was recommended to cut as close to the scalp of the occipital area as possible.

Hair sample of 75 mg was weighed into 50 ml plastic tube, and washed with acetone and then with 0.01% Triton solution, as recommended by the Hair Analysis Standardization Board[54]. The washed hair sample was mixed with 10 ml 6.25% tetra-methyl ammonium hydroxide (TMAH, Tama Chemical, Kawasaki, Japan) and 50 μl 0.1% gold solution (SPEX Certi Prep, Metuchen, NJ, USA), and then dissolved at 75 centigrade with shaking for 2 hours. After cooling the solution to room temperature, internal standard (scandium, gallium and indium) solution was added, and after adjusting its volume gravimetric, the obtained solution was used for multi-mineral analysis. The trace element concentrations were determined with inductively coupled plasma mass spectrometry (ICP-MS; 7500ce, Agilent Technologies, Santa Clara, CA, USA) as reported previously[19,20] and expressed as ng/g hair (ppb) or μg/g hair (ppm). Human hair certified reference material (NIES CRM No. 13) was used to check for the accuracy of analysis. The inter-daily variation of zinc, magnesium, calcium, aluminium, cadmium, lead, mercury and arsenic determination was 2.2, 9.6, 6.3, 8.2, 6.9, 11.1, 9.4 and 6.9%. The control geometric mean value and reference range for each trace element was obtained from the data for 436 male healthy subjects aged 21–40-year-old, as previously reported[19,20,25].

This study has been approved by review of the ethical committee of La Belle Vie Research Laboratory. All of the data obtained are held securely in such a form as to ensure anonymity.

Statistical analysis. Because each trace element concentration in scalp hair was almost log-normally distributed, the mineral concentration was converted to logarithm, and the geometric rather than arithmetic mean is used as representative of its hair concentration. The relation between age and zinc/magnesium concentration of the subjects was examined by Pearson's correlation coefficient test.

References

1. Weintraub, K. Autism counts. *Nature* 479, 22–24 (2011).
2. Pinto, D. *et al*. Functional impact of global rare copy number variation in autism spectrum disorders. *Nature* 466, 368–372 (2010).
3. Chakrabarti, S. & Fombonne, E. Pervasive developmental disorders in preschool children: confirmation of high prevalence. *Am. J. Psychiatry* 162, 1133–1141 (2005).
4. Hughes, V. Autism: Complex disorder. *Nature* 491, S2–S3 (2012).
5. Bailey, A. *et al*. Autism as a strongly genetic disorder: evidence from a British twin study. *Psychol. Med.* 25, 63–77 (1995).
6. Marshall, C. R. *et al*. Structural variation of chromosomes in autism spectrum disorder. *Am. J. Hum. Genet.* 82, 477–488 (2008).
7. Dufault, R. *et al*. Mercury exposure, nutritional deficiencies and metabolic disruption may affect learning in children. *Behav. Brain Funct.* 5, 44–58 (2009).
8. O'Rahilly, S. Human genetics illuminates the paths to metabolic disease. *Nature* 462, 307–314 (2009).
9. Jin, Y. H. *et al*. Cadmium is a mutagen that acts by inhibiting mismatch repair. *Nat. Genet.* 34, 239–241 (2003).
10. Takiguchi, M., Achanzar, W. E., Qu, W., Li, G. & Waalkes, M. P. Effects of cadmium on DNA-(cytosine-5) methyltransferase activity and DNA methylation status during cadmium-induced cellular transformation. *Exp. Cell Res.* 286, 355–365 (2003).
11. Arita, A. & Costa, M. Epigenetics in metal carcinogenesis: nickel, arsenic, chromium and cadmium. *Metallomics* 1, 222–228 (2009).
12. Perera, F. & Herbstman, J. Prenatal environmental exposure, epigenetics, and disease. *Reprod. Toxicol.* 31, 363–373 (2011).
13. Jakovcevski, M. & Akbarian, S. Epigenetic mechanisms in neurological

disease. *Nat. Med.* 18, 1194–1204 (2012).

14. Rodushkin, I. & Axelsson, M. D. Application of double focusing sector field ICP- MS for multi elemental characterization of human hair and nails. Part I. Analytical methodology. *Sci. Total Environ.* 250, 83–100 (2000).

15. Goulle, J. P. *et al.* Metal and metalloid multi-elementary ICP-MS validation in whole blood, plasma, urine and hair: Reference values. *Forens. Sci. Intern.* 153, 39–44 (2005).

16. Wang, C. T., Chang, W. T., Zeng, W. F. & Lin, C. H. Concentrations of calcium, copper, iron, magnesium, potassium, sodium and zinc in adult female hair with different body mass indexes in Taiwan. *Clin. Chem. Lab. Med.* 43, 389–393 (2005).

17. Munakata, M. *et al.* A preliminary analysis of trace elements in the scalp hair of patients with severe motor disabilities receiving enteral nutrition. *Brain Development* 28, 521–525 (2006).

18. Yasuda, H., Yonashiro, T., Yoshida, K., Ishii, T. & Tsutsui, T. Mineral imbalance in children with autistic disorders. *Biomed. Res. Trace Elem.* 16, 285–291 (2005).

19. Yasuda, H., Yonashiro, T., Yoshida, K., Ishii, T. & Tsutsui, T. Relationship between body mass index and minerals in male Japanese adults. *Biomed. Res. Trace Elem.* 17, 316–321 (2006).

20. Yasuda, H. *et al.* Metallomics study using hair mineral analysis and multiple logistic regression analysis: relationship between cancer and minerals. *Environ. Health Prev. Med.* 14, 261–266 (2009).

21. Ochi, A. *et al.* Elemental concentrations in scalp hair, nutritional status and health-related quality of life in haemodialysis patients. *Therap. Apheresis Dialysis* 16, 127–133 (2012).

22. Yasuda, H., Yonashiro, T., Yoshida, K., Ishii, T. & Tsutsui, T. High toxic metal levels in scalp hair of infants and children. *Biomed. Res. Trace Elem.* 16, 39–45 (2005).

23. Yasuda, H., Yoshida, K., Segawa, M., Tokuda, R., Yasuda, Y. & Tsutsui, T. High accumulation of aluminium in hairs of infants and children. *Biomed. Res. Trace Elem.* 19, 57–62 (2008).

24. Yasuda, H., Yoshida, K., Yasuda, Y. & Tsutsui, T. Two age-related accumulation profiles of toxic metals. *Cur. Aging Sci.* 5, 105–111 (2012).

25. Yasuda, H., Yoshida, K., Yasuda, Y. & Tsutsui, T. Infantile zinc deficiency: Association with autism spectrum disorders. *Sci. Rep.* 1, 129; DOI:10.1038/srep00129 (2011).

26. Prasad, A. S. Impact of the discovery of human zinc deficiency on health. *J. Am. Coll. Nutr.* 28, 257–265 (2009).

27. Arnold, L. E. & DiSilvestro, R. A. Zinc in attention-deficit/ hyperactivity disorder. *J. Child Adolesc. Psychopharmacol.* 15, 619–627 (2005).

28. DiGirolamo, A. M. & Raminez-Zea, M. Role of zinc in maternal and child mental health. *Am. J. Clin. Nutr.* 89 (suppl), 940S–945S (2009).

29. Scheplyagina, L. A. Impact of the mother's zinc deficiency on the woman's and new-borns health status. *J. Trace Elem. Med. Biol.* 19, 29–35 (2005).

30. Plum, L. M., Rink, L. & Haase, H. The essential toxin: Impact of zinc on human health. *Intern. J. Environ. Res. Public Health*, 7, 1342–1365 (2010).

31. Dufault, R., Lukiw, W. J., Crider, R., Schnoll, R., Wallinga, D. & Deth, R. A macroepigenetic approach to identify factors responsible for the autism epidemic in the United States. *Clin. Epigenetics* 4, 6 (2012).

32. Yorbik, O., Akay, C., Sayal, A., Cansever, A., Sohmen, T. & Cavdar, A. O. Zinc status in autistic children. *J. Trace Elem. Exp. Med.* 17, 101–107 (2004).

33. Fido, A. & Al-Saad, S. Toxic trace elements in the hair of children with autism. *Autism* 9, 290–298 (2005).

34. Adams, J. B., Holloway, C. E., George, F. & Quig, D. Analyses of toxic metals and essential minerals in the hair of Arizona children with autism and associated conditions, and their mothers. *Biol. Trace Elem. Res.* 110, 193–209 (2006).

35. Faber, S., Zinn, G. M., Kern, J. C. & Kingston, H. M. The plasma zinc/serum copper ratio as a biomarker in children with autism spectrum disorders. *Biomarkers* 14, 171–180 (2009).

36. Lakshmi Priya, M. D. & Geetha, A. Level of trace elements (copper, zinc, magnesium and selenium) and toxic elements (lead and mercury) in the hair and nail of children with autism. *Biol. Trace Elem. Res.* 142, 148–158 (2011).

37. Arnold, L. E. *et al.* Serum zinc correlates with parent- and teacher- rated inattention in children with attention-deficit/hyperactivity disorder. *J. Child Adoles. Psychopharmacol.* 15, 628–636 (2005).

38. Yorbik, O., Ozdag, M. F., Olgun, A., Senol, M. G., Bek, S. & Akman, S. Potential effects of zinc on information processing in boys with attention deficit hyperactivity disorder. *Progr. Neuropsychopharmacol. Biol. Psychiatry* 32, 662–667 (2008).

39. DiGirolamo, A. M. *et al.* Randomized trial of the effect of zinc supplementation on the mental health of school-age children in Guatemala. *Am. J. Clin. Nutr.* 92, 1241–1250 (2010).

40. Akhondzadeh, S., Mohammadi, M. R. & Khademi, M. Zinc sulfate as an adjunct to methylphenidate for the treatment of attention deficit hyperactivity disorder in children: a double blind and randomized trial [ISRCTN64132371].

BMC Psychiatry, 4, 9–14 (2004).

41. Kozielec, T. & Starobrat-Hermelin, B. Assessment of magnesium levels in children with attention deficit hyperactivity disorder (ADHD). *Magnes. Res.* 10, 143–148 (1997).

42. Starobrat-Hermelin, B. & Kozielec, T. The effects of magnesium physiological supplementation on hyperactivity in children with attention deficit hyperactivity disorder (ADHD). Positive response to magnesium oral loading test. *Magnes. Res.* 10, 149–156 (1997).

43. Mousain-Bose, M., Roche, M., Rapin, J. & Bali, J. P. Magnesium VitB6 intake reduces central nervous system hyperexcitability in children. *J. Am. Coll. Nutr.* 23, 545S–548S (2004).

44. Mousain-Bose, M., Roche, M., Polge, A., Pradal-Prat, D., Rapin, J. & Bali, J. P. Improvement of neurobehavioral disorders in children supplemented with magnesium-vitanin B6 II. Pervasive developmental disorder-autism. *Magnes. Res.* 19, 53–62 (2006).

45. Van der Meer, J. M. *et al.* Are autism spectrum disorder and attention-deficit/ hyperactivity disorder different manifestations of one overarching disorder? Cognitive and symptom evidence from a clinical and population-based sample. *J. Am. Acad. Child Adolesc. Psychiatry* 51, 1160–1172 (2012).

46. Dufner-Beattie, J., Kuo, Y. M., Gitschier, J. & Andrews, G. K. The adaptive response to dietary zinc in mice involves the differential cellular localization and zinc regulation of the zinc transporters ZIP4 and ZIP5. *J. Biol. Chem.* 279, 49082–49090 (2004).

47. Lichten, L. A. & Cousins, R. J. Mammalian zinc transporters: nutritional and physiologic regulation. *Ann. Rev. Nutr.* 29, 153–176 (2009).

48. Goyer, R. A. Toxic and essential metal interactions. *Ann. Rev. Nutr.* 17, 37–50 (1997).

49. Razagui, I. B. & Ghribi, I. Maternal and neonatal scalp hair concentrations of zinc, cadmium, and lead: relationship to some lifestyle factors. *Biol. Trace Elem. Res.* 106, 1–28 (2005).

50. Symanski, E. & Hertz-Picciotto, I. Blood lead levels in relation to menopause, smoking, and pregnancy history. *Am. J. Epidemiol.* 141, 1047–1058 (1995).

51. Gulson, B. L., Jameson, C. W., Mahaffey, K. R., Mizon, K. J., Korsch, M. J. & Vimpani, G. Pregnancy increases mobilization of lead from maternal skeleton. *J. Lab. Clin. Med.* 130, 51–62 (1997).

52. Sanders, A. P. *et al.* Towards prenatal biomonitoring in North Carolina: Assessing arsenic, cadmium, mercury and lead levels in pregnant women. *PLoS ONE* 7, e31354 (2012).

53. Eklund, G. & Oskarsson, A. Exposure of cadmium from infant formulas and weaning foods. *Food Addit. Contam.* 16, 509–519 (1999).
54. Cranton, E. M., Bland, J. S., Chatt, A., Krakovitz, R. & Wright, J. V. Standardization and interpretation of human hair for elemental concentrations. *J. Holist. Med.* 4, 10–20 (1982).

Acknowledgements

The authors appreciate the autistic subjects and their relatives for collaboration to this study. The authors thank K.Y. and M.S. for their technical contributions to hair trace element analysis.

Author contributions

H.Y. performed this study, analysed the data and wrote the manuscript with the help of Y.Y. and T.T.

Chapter 3:

ASSESSMENT OF INFANTILE MINERAL IMBALANCES IN AUTISM SPECTRUM DISORDERS (ASDs)

(as a Review Article)

published in **Int J Environ Res Public Health 10: 6027-43 (2013).**

Hiroshi Yasuda and **Toyoharu Tsutsui**
La Belle Vie Research Laboratory, Chuo-ku, Tokyo, Japan,

Abstract: The interactions between genes and the environment are now regarded as the most probable explanation for autism. In this review, we summarize the results of a metallomics study in which scalp hair concentrations of 26 trace elements were examined for 1,967 autistic children (1,553 males and 414 females aged 0–15 years-old), and discuss recent advances in our understanding of epigenetic roles of infantile mineral imbalances in the pathogenesis of autism. In the 1,967 subjects, 584 (29.7%) and 347 (17.6%) were found deficient in zinc and magnesium, respectively, and the incidence rate of zinc deficiency was estimated at 43.5% in male and 52.5% in female infantile subjects aged 0–3 years-old. In contrast, 339 (17.2%), 168 (8.5%) and 94 (4.8%) individuals were found to suffer from high burdens of aluminum, cadmium and lead, respectively, and 2.8% or less from mercury and arsenic. High toxic metal burdens were more frequently observed in the infants aged 0–3 years-old, whose incidence rates were 20.6%, 12.1%, 7.5%, 3.2% and 2.3% for aluminum, cadmium, lead, arsenic and mercury, respectively. These findings suggest that infantile zinc- and magnesium-deficiency and/or toxic metal burdens may be critical and induce epigenetic alterations in the genes and genetic regulation mechanisms of neurodevelopment in the autistic children, and demonstrate that a time factor "infantile window" is also critical for neurodevelopment and probably for therapy. Thus, early metallomics analysis may lead to early screening/estimation and treatment/ prevention for the autistic neurodevelopment disorders.
Keywords: autism spectrum disorders; etiology of neurodevelopment disorders; infantile zinc deficiency; toxic metal burdens; metallomics profiles; epigenetic alterations; infantile window

---

Introduction

Autism spectrum disorders (ASDs) are a group of neural development disorders characterized by impairments in social interaction and communication, and by the presence of restricted and repetitive behaviors [1,2]. Clarification of the pathogenesis and effective treatment of ASDs is one of the challenges today. ASDs continue to increase in prevalence up to 1 in 88 children [1–3] and are known to be highly heritable (~90%), and some related genes have been reported [4–8]. However, the underlying genetic determinants are still not clarified [1,9], and the interaction of heritable factors with uncertified lifestyle and environmental factors seem play a significant role in the pathogenesis. For example, organic mercury had been claimed one of environmental candidates causing autistic disorders [10–12], but its relationship remains to be established. Recently, epigenetic alteration of gene expression by environmental factors is considered one of key events in the pathogenesis of genetic diseases [13,14], and some toxic elements such as cadmium and arsenic have been reported to be candidate factors that induce epigenetic alterations [15–19] and neurodevelopmental disorders [20].

Recent great advances in high-sensitive and reliable trace element analysis method using inductively coupled plasma mass spectrometry (ICP-MS) have enabled it to be applied for forensic medical research and estimating chronic toxic metal burden and mineral deficiency in the human body [21,22]. Thus, the clinical application of reliable hair mineral analysis methods based on ICP-MS has been tried to investigate the association of some diseases/symptoms with trace bio-element kinetics including toxic metals and essential minerals [23–28].

For the last seven years, we have examined the association of toxic metal burdens with autistic disorders, and reported that some of the autistic children have suffered from high accumulation of toxic metals such as cadmium, lead or aluminium [29–31], and recently demonstrating the association with infantile zinc deficiency [32,33].

In this overview article in which human scalp hair concentrations of 26 trace elements have been examined for 1,967 children with autistic disorders aged 0–15 years, we demonstrate that many of the patients, especially in the infants aged 0–3 years-old, are suffering from marginal to severe zinc- and magnesium-deficiency and/or high burdens of several toxic metals such as aluminium, cadmium and lead, indicating the presence of a critical term “infantile window” in neurodevelopment and probably for therapy.

Mineral Disorders in Autism

1.1. *Infantile Zinc Deficiency*

The histogram of hair logarithmic zinc concentrations for 1,967 autistic children diagnosed by their physicians was non-symmetric with tailing in lower range, and 584 in 1,967 subjects (29.7%) were found to have a lower zinc concentration than -2 S.D. (standard deviation) level of the reference range (86.3-193 ppm; geometric mean = 129 ppm), estimated as zinc deficiency. The incidence rates of zinc deficiency in the age groups of 0–3, 4–9 and 10–15 years-old were estimated 43.5%, 28.1% and 3.3% in male and 52.5%, 28.7% and 3.5% in female, and a significant correlation of zinc concentration with age ($r = 0.367$, $p < 0.0001$) was observed (Figure 1), suggesting that infants are more liable to zinc deficiency than elder children. The minimum zinc concentration of 10.7 ppm was detected in a 2-year-old boy, corresponding to about 1/12 of the mean reference level. The zinc concentration of only one 0-year-old case (11 months-old) was 173 ppm in the normal range and seem to be a suspected case, because she was suffered from high burdens of aluminium (52.5 ppm), lead (9.1 ppm), iron (12.8 ppm) and copper (134 ppm). There was little marked gender difference in hair zinc concentration and incidence rate of zinc deficiency.

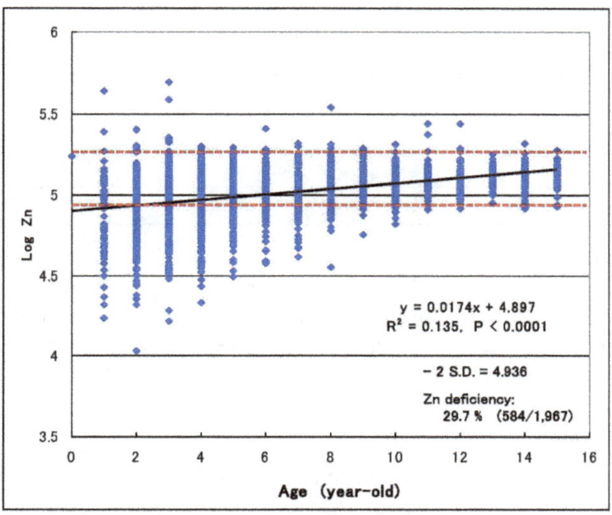

Figure 1. Relation of logarithmic zinc concentration with age in autistic children [33].

The association of hair logarithmic zinc concentration with age in autistic children (N = 1,967) is shown. Each point represents the corresponding age and logarithmic zinc concentration (ng/g hair: ppb) of the individual child. The dotted horizontal lines represent the ±2 S.D. levels of the reference range (86.3–193 ppm) of hair zinc concentrations. A significant relation of the zinc concentration with age ($r = 0.367$, $p < 0.0001$) in the autistic children is shown [33].

1.2. *Infantile Magnesium/Calcium Deficiency*

Following to zinc deficiency, magnesium and calcium deficiency was observed in 347 (17.6%) and 114 (5.8%) individuals in the autistic children, and for the other essential metals such as iron, chromium, manganese, copper and cobalt, their incidence rates of deficiency were 2.0% or less (Table 1). The incidence rates of magnesium deficiency in the age groups of 0–3, 4–9 and 10–15 years-old were 27.0%, 17.1% and 4.2% in male and 22.9%, 12.7% and 4.3% in female subjects, and a significant correlation of magnesium concentration with age ($r = 0.362$, $p < 0.0001$) was observed, suggesting that infants are also liable to magnesium deficiency than elder children. The minimal magnesium concentration of 3.88 ppm was detected in a 2-year-old girl, corresponding to almost 1/10 of the mean reference level (39.5 ppm). Considerable calcium deficiency rate was observed only in lower age groups less than 10 years-old.

Table 1. Prevalence of mineral deficiency in autistic children [33].

Mineral	Number of Cases with Deficiency	Rate (%) of Deficiency
Zn	584	29.7
Mg	347	17.6
Ca	114	5.8
Co	40	2.0
Fe	17	0.9
Cr	12	0.6
Mn	4	0.2
Cu	4	0.2

The number and incidence rate of individuals with mineral deficiency (lower than −2 S.D.) in 1,967 autistic children (1,553 males and 414 females) are shown in the table [33].

1.3. *Toxic Metal Burdens*

In contrast to essential metals, high body burdens of some toxic metals such as aluminium, cadmium and lead of over their +2 S.D. levels were observed in 339 (17.2%), 168 (8.5%) and 94 (4.8%) individuals, respectively, and their incidence rates of high burden were higher than that of mercury and arsenic (2.8% and 2.6%) (Table 2).

Table 2. Prevalence of high toxic metal burden and the maximum level in autistic children				
Toxic Metal	**Number of Cases with High Burden**	**Rate (%) of High Burden**	**Maximum (ppm)**	**Ratio to Reference**
Al	339	17.2	79.4	21.1
Cd	168	8.5	5.5	782.0
Pb	94	4.8	24.9	57.4
Hg	56	2.8	36.3	9.3
As	52	2.6	1.7	33.5

The number and incidence rate of individuals with high toxic metal burden (higher than +2 S.D.) in 1,967 autistic children (1,553 males and 414 females) and the maximum concentration are tabled [33].

High toxic metal burdens were more frequently observed in the infants aged 0–3 years-old: that is, the incidence rate was 20.6%, 12.1%, 7.5%, 3.2% and 2.3% for aluminium, cadmium, lead, arsenic and mercury. The detected maximal concentration of aluminium, cadmium, lead, mercury and arsenic was 79.4 ppm, 5.47 ppm, 24.9 ppm, 36.3 ppm and 1.7 ppm, respectively, corresponding to 21-, 782-, 57-, 9- and 33-fold of each mean reference level.

A high significant inverse relationship between zinc and lead concentrations ($r = -0.339, p < 0.0001$; Figure 2), and also aluminium ($r = -0.247$) and cadmium ($r = -0.198$) concentrations, was observed, suggesting that these toxic metal burdens associate with infantile zinc deficiency.

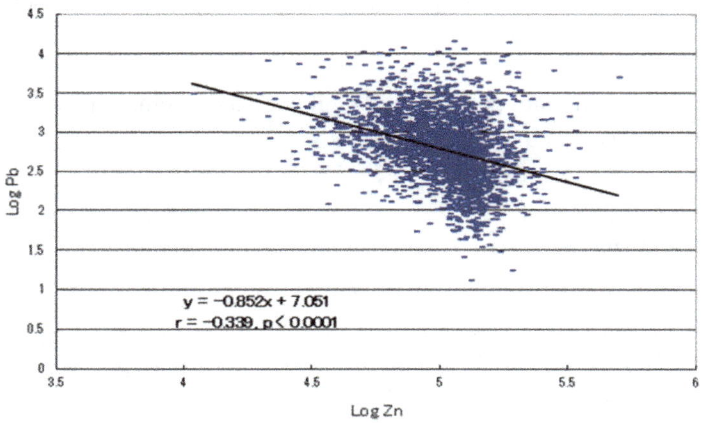

Figure 2. Inverse relation of zinc and lead concentration in autistic children.

The inverse relationship between hair logarithmic zinc and lead concentration in autistic children (N = 1,967) is shown. Each point represents the corresponding logarithmic zinc and lead concentration of the individual child. A high significant inverse relationship between zinc and lead concentrations ($r = -0.339$, $p < 0.0001$) in the autistic children is shown.

Metallomics Profiles in Autistic Infants

There are some sub-types observed in the metallomics profiles characteristic in autistic children. Figure 3 shows a representative autistic profile in a 1-year-old boy suffering from severe zinc- and magnesium-deficiency and simultaneous high burdens of cadmium and lead.

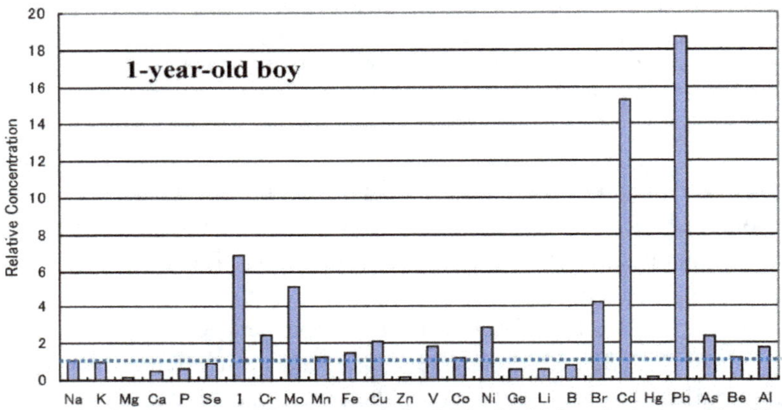

Figure 3. Metallomics profile of an autistic child with high cadmium and lead burdens

A representative metallomics profile of a 1-year-old boy with autism is shown, exhibiting severe zinc- and magnesium-deficiency and simultaneous high burdens with cadmium (107 ppb) and lead (8.11 ppm). Each bar represents the relative concentration of the respective trace element in his scalp hair specimen. The dotted horizontal line at 1.0 represents the reference control level of each trace element [33].

The other autistic metallomics profiles with high burden of aluminium, mercury or arsenic are shown in Figures 4–6.

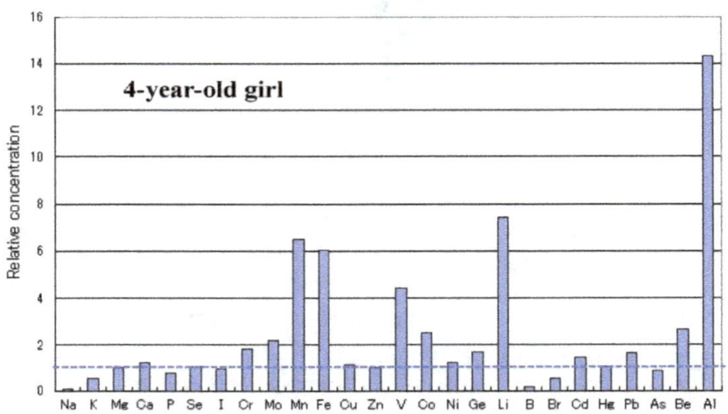

Figure 4. Metallomics profile of an autistic child with high aluminium burden

A representative metallomics profile of 4-year-old girl with autism is shown, exhibiting simultaneous high burdens with aluminium (53.7 ppm), manganese (702 ppb), iron (37.0 ppm) and lithium (12.2 ppb). Each bar represents the relative concentration of the respective trace element in her scalp hair specimen. The dotted horizontal line at 1.0 represents the reference control level of each trace element.

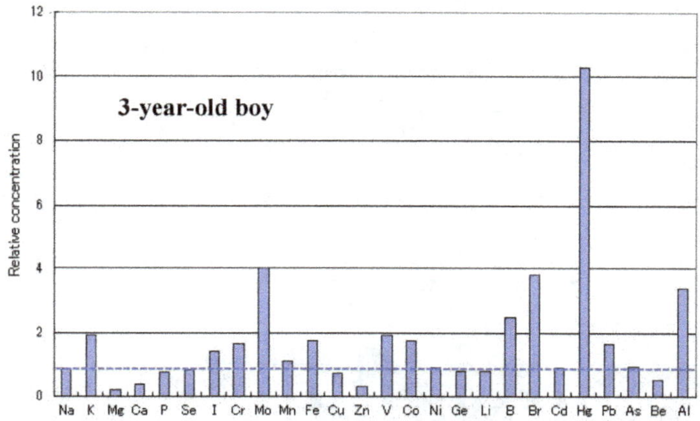

Figure 5. Metallomics profile of an autistic child with high mercury burden.

A metallomics profile of a 3-year-old boy with autism is shown, exhibiting a high burden with mercury of over 10-fold level (40.1 ppm). Each bar represents the relative concentration of the respective trace element in his scalp hair specimen. The dotted horizontal line at 1.0 represents the reference control level of each trace element.

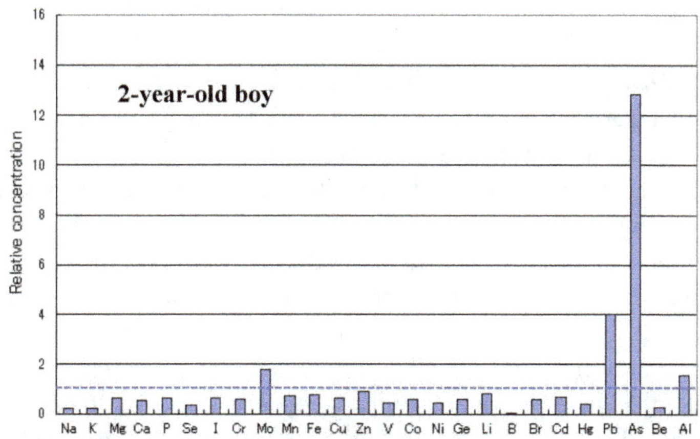

Figure 6. Metallomics profile of an autistic child with high arsenic burden.

A metallomics profile of a 2-year-old boy with autism is shown, exhibiting a high burden with arsenic of over 12-fold level (655 ppb). Each bar represents the relative concentration of the respective trace element in his scalp hair specimen. The dotted horizontal line at 1.0 represents the reference control level of each trace element.

Figure 7 shows a unique metallomics profile with high sodium and potassium concentrations, a characteristic profile detectable in hair specimens. It remains to be clarified which type of various metallome profiles corresponds to which type of autism spectrum disorders.

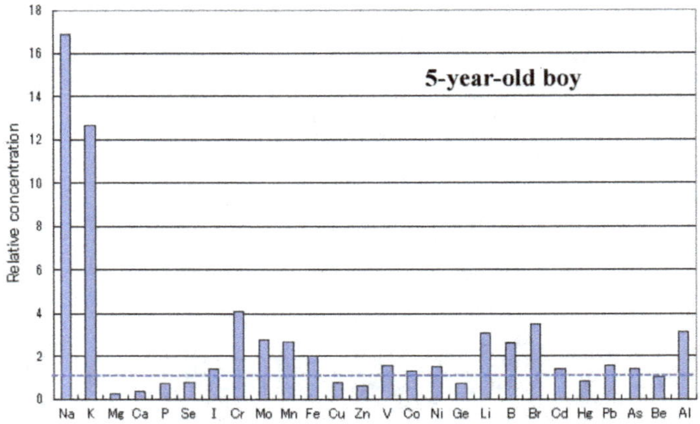

Figure 7. Metallome profile of an autistic child with high sodium and potassium levels. A metallome profile of 5-year-old boy with autism is shown, exhibiting simultaneous high levels of sodium (335 ppm) and potassium (210 ppm). Each bar represents the relative concentration of the respective trace element in his scalp hair specimen. The dotted horizontal line at 1.0 represents the reference control level of each trace element.

1.4. Infantile Time Window in Neurodevelopment and for Therapy

The age at final diagnosis of autism spectrum disorders ranges from 3 to 6 years, although most cases of autism are diagnosed by the age of three and as early as 14 months [34]. In facts, zinc deficiency was detected in many of the infantile patients in the first 3 years of life (Figure 1), and high toxic metal burdens were also detected in the autistic subjects, especially in the younger children (Table 2). Thus, for treatment/prevention of autism spectrum disorders, its early screening and estimation is necessary and it is desirable to early check any metabolic and/or mineral disorders for the infants and children with autistic symptoms, though there are serious limitations of diagnosis of the younger children. It should be considered that the pathogenesis of neurodevelopment disorders might start in prenatal phase and be progressive within the time window for diagnosis.

1.5. Autism-Related Genes and Epigenetic Alteration by Mineral Disorders

Zinc is a structural component of zinc-finger proteins and a transcriptional regulator, and influences some candidate genes reported to be associated with the development of autism, such as MTF1 (metal-responsive transcription factor 1), metallothionein, ZnT5 (zinc transporter 5), COMMD1 (COMM domain-containing protein 1), ERK1 (extracellular signal-regulated kinase 1), TrkB (tyrosine-related kinase B), and ProSAP/Shank (proline-rich synapse-associated protein/SH and multiple ankyrin repeat domains) that themselves are involved in zinc signaling and homeostasis [35–40]. Thus, zinc deficiency observed in the autistic subjects (Figure 1) might induce critical epigenetic alterations to provide a central mechanism of gene/environment interaction to interfere with neuronal maturation during early development [32,38,39].

In addition, high toxic metal burdens detected in the autistic patients (Table 2) might contribute to the mechanism of gene/environment interaction, because cadmium and arsenic have been reported to be candidate factors that induce epigenetic alterations [15–19] and neurodevelopmental disorders [20].

Discussion

In this metallomics study of human scalp hair concentrations of 26 trace elements for 1,967 children with autistic disorders aged 0-15 years, we demonstrate that many of the patients, especially in the infants aged 0-3 years-old, are suffering from marginal to severe zinc- and magnesium- deficiency and/or high burdens of several toxic metals such as aluminium, cadmium and lead.

Zinc is well-accepted as essential trace element that plays important roles in nucleic acid/protein synthesis, cell replication, tissue growth and repair, especially in pregnant women and infants. In fact, zinc ions function as the active centers in more than 300 kinds of enzymes, and about 10% in the total gene-coded proteins have been known to have zinc-finger sequences [38–42], emphasizing the physiological importance of this trace element. In brain, especially in the hippocampus, zinc is co-stored with glutamate in pre-synaptic vesicles in the excitatory neuron terminal, is released from them and controls the activity of excitatory glutamate receptors on the post-synaptic excitable membrane [43,44]. Thus, zinc deficiency is known associated with not only various pathological conditions, including dysgeusia, delayed wound healing, impaired immunity and retarded growth, but also neurodegenerative diseases and neurodevelopment disorders [45–49].

Recently we reported that many infants with autistic disorders are suffering from marginal to severe zinc deficiency, suggesting considerable relationship of infantile zinc deficiency with autism [32]. Furthermore, we have determined scalp hair concentrations of 26 trace elements for 1,967 subjects with autism spectrum disorders and demonstrated that infantile autistic children are liable to deficiency in magnesium and calcium next to zinc, but not in the other essential metals (Table 1) [33]. These findings suggest that autistic infants and probably infants generally have a characteristic liability to zinc- and magnesium-deficiency, because larger amounts of the essential metals (per kg body weight) are needed for the development and growth.

There are numerous studies with the same theme reporting nutritional status and mineral deficiencies in autistic children [50-54]. However, the conclusions of their studies, in which the restricted age (over 4-years-old) of children and number of minerals were examined, were not consistent, and the critical environmental factors remained to be established. In our metallomics analysis study for the 1,967 autistic children aged 0-15 years-old, we were able to demonstrate not only the critical and environmental epigenetic factor (zinc- and magnesium-deficiency and high burdens of aluminium, cadmium, lead and so on) but also the presence of another critical factor, "infantile window" in neurodevelopment and probably for therapy [32,33].

Recently, Gebremedhin *et al.* [55] reported that compared to pregnant women aged 15–24 years, those aged 25–34 and 35–49 years had 1.57 (95% CL: 1.04–2.34) and 2.18 (95% CL: 1.25–3.63) times higher risk of zinc deficiency, respectively. Their study may demonstrate that old age pregnancy is negatively associated to zinc status, maybe suggesting that one of the origins of the high incidence rate of infantile zinc deficiency may be higher age pregnancy of their mothers. Recently, Kurita *et al.* [56] reported that zinc deficiency in utero induces fetal epigenetic alterations of histone modifications in metallothionein 2 promoter region having metal responsive elements in 1-day-old and 5-week-old mice, of which pregnant mother were fed low zinc diet from gestation day 8 until delivery.

Arnold *et al.* [57] reported that mean serum zinc level in children was significantly lower in attention-deficit/hyperactivity disorder (ADHD) group, and that serum zinc level correlated inversely with parent- and teacher-rated inattention in ADHD children. Furthermore, zinc treatment was reported significantly superior to placebo in reducing symptoms of hyperactivity, impulsivity and impaired socialization in ADHD patients [58,59]. Another preliminary human study showed that many children with ADHD have lower zinc concentration in comparison to healthy children and zinc supplement as an adjunct to methylphenidate has favorable effects in the treatment of ADHD children, pointing to the possible association of zinc deficiency and ADHD pathophysiology [60].

Kozielec *et al.* [61] have reported that in 116 hyperactive children with ADHD, magnesium deficiency was found in 95% of the subjects, most frequently in hair (77.6%), next in red-blood cells (58.6%) and in blood serum (33.6%). Furthermore, they reported that in the group of ADHD children given 6 months of magnesium supplementation, a significant decrease of hyperactivity and increase in hair magnesium contents has been achieved [62].

Mousain-Bosc *et al.* [63] also reported that 52 hyper-excitable children have low intra-erythrocyte magnesium levels with normal serum magnesium values, and that magnesium/vitamin B6 supplementation can restore the erythrocyte magnesium levels to normal and improve their abnormal behaviors. They also reported that thirty-three children with clinical symptoms of pervasive developmental disorder or autism (PDD) exhibit significantly lower red blood cell magnesium values, and that the combination therapy with magnesium/vitamin B6 for 6 months improved significantly PDD symptoms in 23/33 children ($p < 0.0001$) with concomitant increases in intra-erythrocyte magnesium values [64].

Recently, Ochi *et al.* [65] found that hair magnesium concentration, but not its serum level, was significantly ($p < 0.01$) inversely-associated with left ventricular hypertrophy in hemodialysis patients, suggesting that hair magnesium concentration is a useful intracellular biomarker independent of its serum level. In a preliminary metallomics study for healthy volunteers, we have observed a high significant correlation between whole blood levels and scalp hair levels of trace elements, but little relation between their serum levels and whole blood levels (unpublished observation). These findings suggest that as biomarker specimen representing mineral dynamics in human body, whole blood or erythrocyte and hair samples are superior to extra-cellular fluids such as serum or plasma for metallomics analysis, although it is necessary to consider that there is a problem of contamination of some trace-elements due to artificial hair treatment such as permanent and coloring.

Recently, dietary restriction-induced zinc deficiency has been reported to up-regulate intestinal zinc-importer (ZIP4) and induce the increase in ZIP4 protein located to the plasma membrane of enterocytes [66,67]. This adoptive response to zinc deficiency is known to lead to increasing in the risk of high-uptake of toxic metals such as cadmium and lead [68]. Thus, infants with zinc deficiency are liable to increased risk of absorbing high amounts of toxic metals and retaining them in their bodies, as shown in Figure 4, which demonstrates a high significant inverse relationship between zinc and lead level. These findings suggest that the increased toxic metal burdens concomitant with zinc deficiency may also epigenetically contribute to the pathogenesis of this disorder.

Deficiency in magnesium/calcium seems further enhance the toxic effects of lead (Pb) on cognitive and behavioral development in children [69]. A significant inverse relationship between dietary calcium intake and blood lead concentrations was found in 3,000 American children examined as part of NHANES II [69]. Elevated blood lead levels are found in some children diagnosed with autism and are associated with the development of ADHD [70,71].

About 250,000 children in the U.S.A. were reported to have high blood lead (Pb) levels over the current Level of Concern of 10 μg/dL [72], despite significant progresses over the past half century in reducing child lead poisoning rates [73]. Therefore, the U.S. Centers for Disease Control and Prevention (CDC) has lowered the Level of Concern from 10 μg/dL to 5 μg/dL [74]. This major change in national policy is based on a large and growing body of evidence showing that even single-digit blood Pb levels have significant impacts on Intelligence Quotients, risks for Attention Deficit Hyperactivity Disorder (ADHD), cardiovascular disease, and kidney function [75-79].

The most common lead exposure pathway for children is ingestion or inhalation of lead-bearing road dusts, whether in the household or outdoor environment [80-82], and its most common sources are fossil fuels, asphalt and paints (lead chromate or lead carbonate) [82-84]. In addition, maternal cigarette smoking has been reported to be associated with lower zinc and higher cadmium and lead concentrations in their neonates [85,86]. These toxic metals accumulated in the maternal bone tissues are co-transferred with calcium to fetal and new-born bodies through activated bone-resorption during pregnancy and lactation [85-88]. In fact, a recent birth cohort study for new-borne in Nepal shows that the motor cluster score was inversely associated with the cord blood levels of lead and arsenic, suggesting that high exposures to Pb and As during the prenatal period may induce retardation during in-utero neurodevelopment [89].

For mercury and arsenic, the maximum burden levels of 9.3- and 33.5-fold of the reference level (Table 2) may also epigenetically play a pathogenic role in the respective autistic individuals, even though their incidence rates were 2.8% or less. It remains to be established that these mineral disorders induce the epigenetic deficits in autism-related candidate genes. In near future, we hope it will be clarified what type of metallomics profiles is associated with what disorder in various behavior/neurological deficits in autism spectrum disorders.

It is demonstrated that many autistic infants are suffering from marginal to severe zinc- and magnesium-deficiency and/or high toxic metal burdens of aluminium, cadmium, lead and so on. These findings suggest that infantile autistic patients with mineral disorders may respond to a novel evidence-based nutritional approach which supplements deficient nutrients and detoxifies accumulated toxic metals. This evidence-based nutritional approach may yield a new vista into early screening/assessment and treatment/prevention of infantile patients with autism spectrum disorders including the suspects. Well-controlled intervention studies for this novel nutritional therapy are desired to establish the epigenetic roles of infantile mineral imbalances in the pathogenesis of neurodevelopment disorders and to develop an early screening and therapy of neurodevelopment disorders such as autism spectrum disorders, ADHD and learning disorder.

Conclusions

This overview demonstrates that many of infantile patients with autism spectrum disorders suffer from marginal to severe zinc- and magnesium-deficiency and/or high toxic metal burdens, and that these mineral disorders (mineral imbalances) in bodies may play principal, epigenetic roles as environment factors in the pathogenesis of the neurodevelopment disorders. In addition, it is suggested that there is a critical time window "infantile window" in neurodevelopment and probably for treatment and prevention of these disorders. In near future, an introduction of innovative clinical tests such as metabolomics and metallomics analysis is desired for early estimation and treatment of neurodevelopment disorders.

Acknowledgments

The authors appreciate the autistic subjects and their relatives for collaboration to this study.

References

1. Weintraub, K. Autism counts. *Nature* **2011**, *479*, 22-24.
2. Pinto, D.; Pagnamenta, A.T.; Klei, L.; Anney, R.; Merico, D.; Regan, R.; Conroy, J.; Magalhaes, T.R.; Correia, C.; Abrahams, B.S.; *et al.* Functional impact of global rare copy number variation in autism spectrum disorders. *Nature* **2010**, *466*, 368-372.
3. Chakrabarti, S.; Fombonne, E. Pervasive developmental disorders in preschool children: Confirmation of high prevalence. *Amer. J. Psychiat.* **2005**, *162*, 1133-1141.
4. Bailey, A.; le Couteur, A.; Gottesman, I.; Bolton, P.; Simonoff, E.; Yuzda, E.; Rutter, M. Autism as a strongly genetic disorder: Evidence from a British twin study. *Psychol. Med.* **1995**, *25*, 63-77.
5. Marshall, C.R.; Noor, A.; Vincent, J.B.; Lionel, A.C.; Feuk, L.; Skaug, J.; Shago, M.; Moessner, R.; Pinto, D.; Ren, Y.; *et al.* Structural variation of chromosomes in autism spectrum disorder. *Amer. J. Hum. Genet.* **2008**, *82*, 477-488.

6. Kim, S.J.; Silva, R.M.; Flores, C.G.; Jacob, S.; Guter, S.; Valcante, G.; Zaytoun, A.M.; Cook, E.H.; Badner, J.A. A quantitative association study of SLC25A12 and restricted repetitive behavior traits in autism spectrum disorders. *Mol. Autism* **2011**, *2*, doi:10.1186/2040-2392-2-8.

7. Murdoch, J.D.; State, M.W. Recent developments in the genetics of autism spectrum disorders. *Curr. Opin. Genet. Dev.* **2013**, *23*, 310-315.

8. Huguet, G.; Ey, E.; Bourgeron, T. The genetic landscapes of autism spectrum disorders. *Ann. Rev. Genomics Hum. Genet.* **2013**, *14*, 191-213.

9. Hughes, V. Autism: Complex disorder. *Nature* **2012**, *491*, S2-S3.

10. Dufault, R.; Schnoll, R.; Lukiw, W.J.; Leblanc, B.; Cornett, C.; Patrick, L.; Wallinga, D.; Gilbert, S.G.; Crider, R. Mercury exposure, nutritional deficiencies and metabolic disruption may affect learning in children. *Behav. Brain Funct.* **2009**, *5*, 44-58.

11. Palmer, R.F.; Blanchard, S.; Wood, R. Proximity to point sources of environmental mercury release as a predictor of autism prevalence. *Health Place* **2009**, *15*, 18-24.

12. Majewska, M.D.; Urbanowicz, E.; Rok-Bujko, P.; Namyslowska, I.; Mierzejewsky, P. Age-dependent lower or higher levels of hair mercury in autistic children than in healthy controls. *Acta Neurobiol. Exp.* **2010**, *70*, 196-208.

13. O'Rahilly, S. Human genetics illuminates the paths to metabolic disease. *Nature* **2009**, *462*, 307-314.

14. James, S.J.; Shpyleva, S.; Melnyk, S.; Pavliv, O.; Pogribny, I.P. Complex epigenetic regulation of engrailed-2 (EN-2) homeobox gene in the autism cerebellum. *Transl. Psychiat.* **2013**, *3*, e232, doi:10.1038/tp.2013.8.

15. Jin, Y.H.; Clark, A.B.; Slebos, R.J.; Al-Refai, H.; Taylor, J.A.; Kunkel, T.A.; Resnick, M.A.; Gordenin, D.A. Cadmium is a mutagen that acts by inhibiting mismatch repair. *Nat. Genet.* **2003**, *34*, 239-241.

16. Takiguchi, M.; Achanzar, W.E.; Qu, W.; Li, G.; Waalkes, M.P. Effects of cadmium on DNA-(cytosine-5) methyltransferase activity and DNA methylation status during cadmium-induced cellular transformation. *Exp. Cell Res.* **2003**, *286*, 355-365.

17. Arita, A.; Costa, M. Epigenetics in metal carcinogenesis: Nickel, arsenic, chromium and cadmium. *Metallomics* **2009**, *1*, 222-228.

18. Perera, F.; Herbstman, J. Prenatal environmental exposure, epigenetics, and disease. *Reprod. Toxicol.* **2011**, *31*, 363-373.

19. Jakovcevski, M.; Akbarian, S. Epigenetic mechanisms in neurological disease. *Nat. Med.* **2012**, *18*, 1194-1204.

20. Ciesielski, T.; Weuve, J.; Bellinger, D.C.; Schwartz, J.; Lanphear, B.; Wright,

R.O. Cadmium exposure and neurodevelopmental outcomes in U.S. children. *Environ. Health Perspect.* **2012**, *120*, 758-763.

21. Rodushkin, I.; Axelsson, M.D. Application of double focusing sector field ICP-MS for multi elemental characterization of human hair and nails. Part I. Analytical methodology. *Sci. Total Environ.* **2000**, *250*, 83-100.

22. Goulle, J.P.; Mahieu, L.; Castermant, J.; Neveu, N.; Bonneau, L.; Lainé, G.; Bouige, D.; Lacroix, C. Metal and metalloid multi-elementary ICP-MS validation in whole blood, plasma, urine and hair: Reference values. *Forensic Sci. Int.* **2005**, *153*, 39-44.

23. Wang, C.T.; Chang, W.T.; Zeng, W.F.; Lin, C.H. Concentrations of calcium, copper, iron, magnesium, potassium, sodium and zinc in adult female hair with different body mass indexes in Taiwan. *Clin. Chem. Lab. Med.* **2005**, *43*, 389-393.

24. Munakata, M.; Onuma, A.; Kobayashi, Y.; Haginoya, K.; Yokoyama, H.; Fujiwara, I.; Yasuda, H.; Tsutsui, T.; Iinuma, K. A preliminary analysis of trace elements in the scalp hair of patients with severe motor disabilities receiving enteral nutrition. *Brain Dev.* **2006**, *28*, 521-525.

25. Yasuda, H.; Yonashiro, T.; Yoshida, K.; Ishii, T.; Tsutsui, T. Mineral imbalance in children with autistic disorders. *Biomed. Res. Trace Elem.* **2005**, *16*, 285-291.

26. Yasuda, H.; Yonashiro, T.; Yoshida, K.; Ishii, T.; Tsutsui, T. Relationship between body mass index and minerals in male Japanese adults. *Biomed. Res. Trace Elem.* **2006**, *17*, 316-321.

27. Yasuda, H.; Yoshida, K.; Segawa, M.; Tokuda, R.; Tsutsui, T.; Yasuda, Y.; Magara, S. Metallomics study using hair mineral analysis and multiple logistic regression analysis: Relationship between cancer and minerals. *Environ. Health Prev. Med.* **2009**, *14*, 261-266.

28. Ochi, A.; Ishimura, E.; Tsujimoto, Y.; Kakiya, R.; Tabata, T.; Mori, K.; Tahara, H.; Shoji, T.; Yasuda, H.; Nishizawa, Y.; *et al.* Elemental concentrations in scalp hair, nutritional status and health-related quality of life in haemodialysis patients. *Ther. Apher. Dial.* **2012**, *16*, 127–133.

29. Yasuda, H.; Yonashiro, T.; Yoshida, K.; Ishii, T.; Tsutsui, T. High toxic metal levels in scalp hair of infants and children. *Biomed. Res. Trace Elem.* **2005**, *16*, 39–45.

30. Yasuda, H.; Yoshida, K.; Segawa, M.; Tokuda, R.; Yasuda, Y.; Tsutsui, T. High accumulation of aluminium in hairs of infants and children. *Biomed. Res. Trace Elem.* **2008**, *19*, 57-62.

31. Yasuda, H.; Yoshida, K.; Yasuda, Y.; Tsutsui, T. Two age-related accumulation profiles of toxic metals. *Curr. Aging Sci.* **2012**, *5*, 105-111.

32. Yasuda, H.; Yoshida, K.; Yasuda, Y.; Tsutsui, T. Infantile zinc deficiency: Association with autism spectrum disorders. *Sci. Rep.* **2011**, *1*, 00129. doi:10.1038/srep00129.

33. Yasuda, H.; Yasuda, Y.; Tsutsui, T. Estimation of autistic children by metallomics analysis. *Sci. Rep.* **2013**, *3*, 01199. doi:10.1038/srep01199.

34. Landa, R.J. Diagnosis of autism spectrum disorders in the first 3 years of life. *Nat. Clin. Pract. Neurol.* **2008**, *4*, 138-147.

35. Huang, Y.Z.; Pan, E.; Xiong, Z.Q.; McNamara, J.O. Zinc-mediated transactivation of TrkB potentiates the hippocampal mossy fiber-CA3 pyramidal synapse. *Neuron* **2008**, *57*, 546-558.

36. O'Roak, B.J.; Deriziotis, P.; Lee, C.; Vives, L.; Schwartz, J.J.; Girirajan, S.; Karakoc, E.; Mackenzie, A.P.; Ng, S.B.; Baker, C.; *et al.* Exome sequencing in sporadic autism spectrum disorders identifies severe *de novo* mutations. *Nat. Genet.* **2011**, *43*, 585-589.

37. Sanders, S.J.; Murtha, M.T.; Gupta, A.R.; Murdoch, J.D.; Raubeson, M.J.; Willsey, A.J.; Ercan-Sencicek, A.G.; DiLullo, N.M.; Parikshak, N.N.; Stein, J.L.; *et al. De novo* mutations revealed by whole exome sequencing are strongly associated with autism. *Nature* **2012**, *485*, 237-241.

38. Grabrucker, A.M. Environmental factors in autism. *Front. Psychist.* **2013**, *3*, 1-13.

39. Dufault, R.; Lukiw, W.J.; Crider, R.; Schnoll, R.; Wallinga, D.; Deth, R. A macroepigenetic approach to identify factors responsible for the autism epidemic in the United States. *Clin. Epigenetics* **2012**, *4*, 6, doi:10.1186/1868-7083-4-6.

40. Grabrucker, A.M. A role for synaptic zinc in ProSAP/Shank PSD scaffold malformation in autism spectrum disorders. *Dev. Neurobiol.* **2013**, doi:10.1002/dneu.22089.

41. Fukada, T.; Yamasaki, S.; Nishida, K.; Murakami, M.; Hirano, T. Zinc homeostasis and signalling in health and diseases: Zinc signalling. *J. Biol. Inorg. Chem.* **2011**, *16*, 1123-1134.

42. Andreini, C.; Banci, L.; Bertini, I.; Rosato, A. Counting the zinc-proteins encoded in the human genome. *J. Proteome Res.* **2006**, *5*, 196-201.

43. Takeda, A. Movement of zinc and its functional significance in the brain. *Brain Res. Rev.* **2000**, *34*, 137-148.

44. Takeda, A.; Nakamura, M.; Fujii, H.; Tamano, H. Synaptic Zn^{2+} homeostasis and its significance. *Metallomics* **2013**, *5*, 417-423.

45. Prasad, A.S. Impact of the discovery of human zinc deficiency on health. *J. Am. Coll. Nutr.* **2009**, *28*, 257-265.

46. Arnold, L.E.; di Silvestro, R.A. Zinc in attention-deficit/hyperactivity disorder. *J. Child Adolesc. Psychopharmacol.* **2005**, *15*, 619-627.
47. di Girolamo, A.M.; Raminez-Zea, M. Role of zinc in maternal and child mental health. *Amer. J. Clin. Nutr.* **2009**, *89*, S940-S945.
48. Scheplyagina, L.A. Impact of the mother's zinc deficiency on the woman's and new-borns health status. *J. Trace Elem. Med. Biol.* **2005**, *19*, 29-35.
49. Plum, L.M.; Rink, L.; Haase, H. The essential toxin: Impact of zinc on human health. *Int. J. Environ. Res. Public Health* **2010**, *7*, 1342-1365.
50. Yorbik, O.; Akay, C.; Sayal, A.; Cansever, A.; Sohmen, T.; Cavdar, A.O. Zinc status in autistic children. *J. Trace Elem. Exp. Med.* **2004**, *17*, 101-107.
51. Fido, A.; Al-Saad, S. Toxic trace elements in the hair of children with autism. *Autism* **2005**, *9*, 290-298.
52. Adams, J.B.; Holloway, C.E.; George, F.; Quig, D. Analyses of toxic metals and essential minerals in the hair of Arizona children with autism and associated conditions, and their mothers. *Biol. Trace Elem. Res.* **2006**, *110*, 193-209.
53. Faber, S.; Zinn, G.M.; Kern, J.C.; Kingston, H.M. The plasma zinc/serum copper ratio as a biomarker in children with autism spectrum disorders. *Biomarkers* **2009**, *14*, 171-180.
54. Priya, M.D.L.; Geetha, A. Level of trace elements (copper, zinc, magnesium and selenium) and toxic elements (lead and mercury) in the hair and nail of children with autism. *Biol. Trace Elem. Res.* **2011**, *142*, 148-158.
55. Gebremedhin, S.; Enquselassie, F.; Umeta, M. Prevalence of prenatal zinc deficiency and its association with socio-demographic, dietary and health care related factors in Rural Sidama, Southern Ethiopia: A cross-sectional study. *BMC Public Health* **2011**, *11*, 898-907.
56. Kurita, H.; Ohsako, S.; Hashimoto, S.; Yoshinaga, J.; Tohyama, C. Prenatal zinc deficiency-dependent epigenetic alterations of mouse metallothionein-2 gene. *J. Nutr. Biochem.* **2013**, *24*, 256-266.
57. Arnold, L.E.; Bozzolo, H.; Hollway, J.; Cook, A.; di Silvestro, R.A.; Bozzolo, D.R.; Crowl, L.; Ramadan, Y.; Williams, C. Serum zinc correlates with parent- and teacher-rated inattention in children with attention-deficit/ hyperactivity disorder. *J. Child Adoles. Psychopharmacol.* **2005**, *15*, 628-636.
58. Yorbik, O.; Ozdag, M.F.; Olgun, A.; Senol, M.G.; Bek, S.; Akman, S. Potential effects of zinc on information processing in boys with attention deficit hyper-activity disorder. *Prog. Neuropsychopharmacol. Biol. Psychiatry* **2008**, *32*, 662-667.
59. di Girolamo, A.M.; Ramirez-Zea, M.; Wang, M.; Flores-Ayala, R.; Martorell, R.; Neufeld, L.M.; Ramakrishnan, U.; Sellen, D.; Black, M.M.; Stein, A.D. Randomized trial of the effect of zinc supplementation on the mental health of

school-age children in Guatemala. *Am. J. Clin. Nutr.* **2010**, *92*, 1241-1250.

60. Akhondzadeh, S.; Mohammadi, M.R.; Khademi, M. Zinc sulfate as an adjunct to methylphenidate for the treatment of attention deficit hyperactivity disorder in children: A double blind and randomised trial [ISRCTN64132371]. *BMC Psychiatry* **2004**, *4*, 9-14.

61. Kozielec, T.; Starobrat-Hermelin, B. Assessment of magnesium levels in children with attention deficit hyperactivity disorder (ADHD). *Magnes. Res.* **1997**, *10*, 143-148.

62. Starobrat-Hermelin, B.; Kozielec, T. The effects of magnesium physiological supplementation on hyperactivity in children with attention deficit hyperactivity disorder (ADHD). Positive response to magnesium oral loading test. *Magnes. Res.* **1997**, *10*, 149-156.

63. Mousain-Bose, M.; Roche, M.; Rapin, J.; Bali, J.P. Magnesium VitB6 intake reduces central nervous system hyperexcitability in children. *J. Amer. Coll. Nutr.* **2004**, *23*, S545-S548.

64. Mousain-Bose, M.; Roche, M.; Polge, A.; Pradal-Prat, D.; Rapin, J.; Bali, J.P. Improvement of neurobehavioral disorders in children supplemented with magnesium-vitanin B6 II. Pervasive developmental disorder-autism. *Magnes. Res.* **2006**, *19*, 53-62.

65. Ochi, A.; Ishimura, E.; Tsujimoto, Y.; Kakiya, R.; Tabata, T.; Mori, K.; Fukumoto, S.; Tahara, H.; Shoji, T.; Yasuda, H.; *et al.* Hair magnesium, but not serum magnesium, is associated with left ventricular wall thickness in hemodialysis patients. *Circ. J.* **2013**, doi:10.1253/circj.CJ-13-0347.

66. Dufner-Beattie, J.; Kuo, Y.M.; Gitschier, J.; Andrews, G.K. The adaptive response to dietary zinc in mice involves the differential cellular localization and zinc regulation of the zinc transporters ZIP4 and ZIP5. *J. Biol. Chem.* **2004**, *279*, 49082-49090.

67. Lichten, L.A.; Cousins, R.J. Mammalian zinc transporters: Nutritional and physiologic regulation. *Ann. Rev. Nutr.* **2009**, *29*, 153-176.

68. Goyer, R.A. Toxic and essential metal interactions. *Ann. Rev. Nutr.* **1997**, *17*, 37-50.

69. Mahaffey, K.R.; Gartside, P.S.; Glueck, C.J. Blood lead levels and dietary calcium intake in 1 to 11 years-old children: The second national health and nutrition examination survey, 1976 to 1980. *Pediatrics* **1986**, *78*, 257-262.

70. Shannon, M.; Graef, J.W. Lead intoxication in children with pervasive developmental disorders. *J. Toxicol. Clin. Toxicol.* **1996**, *34*, 177-181.

71. Eubig, P.A.; Agular, A.; Schantz, S.L. Lead and PCBs as risk factors for attention deficit/hyperactivity disorder. *Environ. Health Perspect.* **2010**, *118*,

1654-1667.
72. Centers for Disease Control and Prevention (CDC). CDC National Surveillance Data (1997–2009), National Centers for Environmental Health 2012. Available online: http://www.cdc.gov/nceh/lead/ data/national.htm. (accessed on 6 November 2013).
73. Jones, R.L.; Homa, D.M.; Meyer, P.A.; Brody, D.J.; Caldwell, K.L.; Pirkle, J.L.; Brown, M.J. Trends in blood lead levels and blood testing among US children aged 1 to 5 years, 1988–2004. *Pediatrics* **2009**, *123*, 376-385.
74. Advisory Committee on Childhood Lead Poisoning Prevention, of the Centers for Disease Control and Prevention (ACCLPP). *Low Level Lead Exposure Harms Children: A Renewed Call for Primary Prevention: Report to the CDCP*; ACCLPP: Atlanta, GA, USA, 2012; pp. 1-54.
75. Needleman, H.L.; Schell, A.; Bellinger, D.; Leviton, A.; Allred, E.N. The long-term effects of exposure to low doses of lead in childhood. An 11-year follow up report. *N. Engl. J. Med.* **1990**, *322*, 83-88.
76. Binns, H.J.; Campbell, C.; Brown, M.J. Interpreting and managing blood lead levels of less than 10 micro g/dL in children and reducing childhood exposure to lead: Recommendations of the centers for disease control and prevention advisory committee on childhood lead poisoning prevention. *Pediatrics* **2007**, *120*, e1285-e1298. doi: 10.1542/peds.2005-1770.
77. Bellinger, D.C. Lead neurotoxicity and socioeconomic status: Conceptual and analytical issues. *Neurotoxicology* **2008**, *29*, 828-832.
78. Gump, B.B.; Stewart, P.; Reihman, J.; Lonky, E.; Darvill, T.; Parsons, P.J.; Granger, D.A. Low-level prenatal and postnatal blood lead (Pb) exposure and adrenocortical responses to acute stress in children. *Environ. Health Perspect.* **2008**, *116*, 249-255.
79. Nigg, J.T.; Knottnerus, G.M.; Martel, M.M.; Nikoas, M.; Cavanagh, V.; Karmaus, W.; Rappley, M.D. Low blood lead levels associated with clinically diagnosed attention-deficit/hyperactivity disorder and mediated by weak cognitive control. *Biol. Psychiatry* **2008**, *63*, 325-331.
80. Dixon, S.L.; Gaitens, J.M.; Jacobs, D.E.; Strauss, W.; Nagaraja, L.; Pivetz, T.; Wilson, J.W.; Ashley, P.J. Exposure of U.S. children to residential dust lead, 1999–2004: II. The contribution of lead-contaminated dust to children's blood lead levels. *Environ. Health Perspect.* **2009**, *117*, 468-474.
81. American Academy of Pediatrics. Lead exposure in children: Prevention, detection, and management: Statement of policy reaffirmation. *Psychiatry* **2009**, *123*, 1421-1422.
82. Deocampo, D.M.; Reed, P.J.; Kalenuik, A.P. Road dust lead (Pb) in two

neighborhoods of urban Atlanta, (GA, USA). *Int. J. Environ. Res. Public Health* **2012**, *9*, 2020-2030.

83. Hall, G.; Tinklenberg, J. Determination of Ti, Zn, and Pb in lead-based house paints by EDXRF. *J. Anal. At. Spectrom.* **2003**, *18*, 775-778.

84. Lewis, P.A. Inorganic Colored Pigments. In *Paint and Coating Testing Manual*, 14th ed.; Koleske, J.V., Ed.; ASTM: West Conshohocken, PA, USA, 1995; pp. 1-950.

85. Symanski, E.; Hertz-Picciotto, I. Blood lead levels in relation to menopause, smoking, and pregnancy history. *Amer. J. Epidemiol.* **1995**, *141*, 1047-1058.

86. Razagui, I.B.; Ghribi, I. Maternal and neonatal scalp hair concentrations of zinc, cadmium, and lead: Relationship to some lifestyle factors. *Biol. Trace Elem. Res.* **2005**, *106*, 1-28.

87. Gulson, B.L.; Jameson, C.W.; Mahaffey, K.R.; Mizon, K.J.; Korsch, M.J.; Vimpani, G. Pregnancy increases mobilization of lead from maternal skeleton. *J. Lab. Clin. Med.* **1997**, *130*, 51-62.

88. Sanders, A.P.; Flood, K.; Chiang, S.; Herring, A.H.; Wolf, L.; Fry, R.C. Towards prenatal biomonitoring in North Carolina: Assessing arsenic, cadmium, mercury and lead levels in pregnant women. *PLoS One* **2012**, *7*, e31354. doi:10.1371/journal.pone.0031354.

89. Parajuli, R.P.; Fujiwara, T.; Umezaki, M.; Watanabe, C. Association of cord blood levels of lead, arsenic, and zinc with neurodevelopmental indicators in newborns: A birth cohort study in Chitwan Valley, Nepal. *Environ. Res.* **2012**, *10*, 509-519.

Chapter 4:

METALLOMICS ANALYSIS FOR ASSESSMENT OF TOXIC METAL BURDENS IN INFANTS/CHILDREN AND THEIR MOTHERS: EARLY ASSESSMENT AND INTERVENTION ARE ESSENTIAL.

published in **Biomolecules 11, 6 (2021)**.

Hiroshi Yasuda [1], **Toyoharu Tsutsui** [1] and **Katsuhiko Suzuki** [2]

[1] La Belle Vie Research Laboratory, Tokyo 103-0006, Japan

[2] Faculty of Sport Sciences, Waseda University, Tokorozawa 359-1192, Japan

Abstract: Accumulation of toxic metals in infants/children is of serious concern worldwide, from the viewpoint of their harmful effects on the normal growth and development. This metallomics study investigates the extent of toxic metal burdens in infants/children and the relationship to those in their mothers for 77 child/mother pair subjects. For mercury, its geometric mean concentration in infants/children was of similar level to that in their mothers, and a high-significant close correlation was observed between infants/children and their mothers ($\beta = 0.758$, $r = 0.539$, $p < 0.0001$). A significant but less intimate mother/child relationship was observed for arsenic ($\beta = 0.301$, $r = 0.433$), lead ($\beta = 0.444$, $r = 0.471$) and aluminum ($\beta = 0.379$, $r = 0.451$). Remarkably, the burden levels of lead, cadmium and aluminum in infants/children were approximately three times higher than those in their mothers ($p < 0.0001$), and the burden levels in some individuals were several tens of times higher than in the mothers. In contrast, some essential metal levels such as zinc, magnesium and calcium in infants/children were significantly lower than those in their mothers, and 29 individuals (37.7%) in the child subjects were estimated to be zinc-deficient. In addition, significant inverse correlations were observed between zinc and lead ($r = -0.267$, $p = 0.019$), and magnesium and arsenic ($r = -0.514$, $p < 0.0001$). These findings suggest that these toxic metal burdens and essential metal deficiencies in infants/children are of serious concern for their neurodevelopment, indicating that the early assessment and intervention are crucial. It is expected that larger epidemiological and intervention studies will provide a reasonable and essential pathway for intervention of neurodevelopment disorders.

Keywords: metallomics analysis; toxic metal burdens; zinc deficiency; metal imbalance; metal-metal correlations; Infantile time window; child/mother relationship; early assessment and intervention

Introduction

Accumulation of toxic metals in infants and children is of serious concern worldwide, from the viewpoint of their harmful effects on normal growth and development of infants and children [1–8]. The pathogenic roles of some toxic metals have been interested in various neurodegenerative diseases [9,10], and mercury, lead, aluminum, and cadmium were reported to cause some fractions of neurodevelopmental disabilities [4–8] and retardation of children's growth [11,12]. In addition, we demonstrated zinc- and magnesium deficiency and toxic metal burdens such as aluminum, cadmium, lead, arsenic and mercury in autistic children [4,5,13,14], particularly in the infantile subjects aged 0–3 years, and statistically significant inverse relationship between zinc and lead, between zinc and cadmium, and between zinc and aluminum concentrations in these children, indicating the presence of "Infantile Time Window" in neurodevelopment disorders and for intervention [4,5,14]. Cusick and Georgirff pointed out the importance of micronutrients including iron and zinc in early childhood before the age of 3 years in brain development [15]. The critical role of zinc deficiency in etiology of autism has been suggested by recent studies that estimated fetal and postnatal exposure profiles of toxic metals and essential minerals [6,7,16], and that investigated AMPA (α-amino-3-hydroxy-5-methyl-4-isoxazolepropionic acid) receptor subunit switch controlled by zinc and Shank in developing neurons [17,18]. Hagmeyer et al. [19] suggested the beneficial effects of zinc supplementation in treatment of autism and Phelan McDermid Syndrome.

This study was undertaken to investigate the incidence and extent of accumulation of toxic metals in infants/children and to examine whether their toxic metal burdens are affected by those in their mothers. In addition, the concentrations of 13-kind essential minerals in the same subjects were determined simultaneously and the possible relationship between toxic metal burden and deficiency in some essential metals was examined.

Materials and Methods

1.1. *Study Subjects*

In collaboration with the Food Safety Citizen's Watch, after obtaining informed consent, 77 pairs of Japanese infants and children (28 males and 49 females; 0-11 years-old) and their mothers were recruited, and their scalp hair samples were collected and used for this study. A hair sample, a kind of cellular body, is widely used as a noninvasive, stable and useful bio-specimen for assessment of environmental exposure of toxic metals, for evaluation of nutritional status and in forensic science [1,3–5,8].

The research protocol for examining exposure to main toxic metals, mercury (Hg), arsenic (As), cadmium (Cd), lead (Pb) and aluminum (Al) and their effects in human health and diseases was approved by the ethical committee of the La Belle Vie research laboratory.

1.2. *Sampling and Metal Analysis*

Hair sampling was conducted by cutting hair as close as possible to the scalp of the occipital area. Scalp hair samples were mailed from the child/mother pair subjects to the laboratory.

A 75 mg hair sample was weighed into a 50 mL plastic tube and washed with acetone and then with a 0.01% Triton solution, in accordance with the procedures recommended by the Hair Analysis Standardization Board, as previously described [3–5]. The washed hair sample was mixed with 10 mL 6.25% tetramethylammonium hydroxide (TMAH, Tama Chemical, Kawasaki, Japan) and 50 μL 0.1% gold solution (SPEX Certi Prep, Metuchen, NJ, USA), and then dissolved at 75 °C with shaking for 2 h. After cooling the solution to room temperature, an internal standard solution was added. After adjusting its volume gravimetrically, the obtained solution was used for metal analysis. The metal concentrations were determined with inductively coupled plasma mass spectrometry (ICP-MS; 7500ce, Agilent Technologies, Santa Clara, CA, USA) by the internal standard method [3–5,13,14] and expressed as ng/g hair (ppb). The reference geometric mean values for each trace element were obtained from the data for 436 male healthy subjects aged 21–40 year-old, as previously reported [4,5,13,20], and used for the calculation of relative concentrations to examine metallome profiles of several pairs of infant/child and mother. All of the data collected were held securely in such a form as to ensure anonymity.

1.3. *Statistical Analysis*

Because scalp hair mineral concentration follows a log-normal distribution, the log of each metal concentration and the geometric rather than arithmetic mean were used to represent the hair metal concentration. Statistical differences between geometric mean con- centration of metals in infants/children and in their mothers were analyzed using Welch's t test. Since there were no significant gender differences in the concentrations of 5-kind toxic metals and 13-kind essential minerals between male and female infants/children (data not shown), the pooled data in a total 77 child subjects was compared with that in their mothers. The relationship of metal concentration between infants/children and their mothers was examined using Pearson's correlation coefficient. The correlation of some metal-metal pairs in infants/children and in mothers was also analyzed by the same method.

Results

Metallomics analysis of 26-kind of trace bio-elements including toxic metals in scalp hair samples of 77 pair subjects of Japanese infants/children (28 males and 49 females; 0-11 years-old; mean age: 5.2 years old) and their mothers (mean age: 38.4 years old) were investigated in this study. Geometric mean concentration of mercury in infants/children was not statistically different from that in their mothers, and a high-significant close correlation ($\beta = 0.758$, $r = 0.539$, $p < 0.0001$) was observed between mothers and infants/children (Figure 1a), suggesting equivalent exposure to mercury in infants/children and mothers. A significant but less intimate mother/child relationship was observed for arsenic ($\beta = 0.301$, $r = 0.433$), lead ($\beta = 0.444$, $r = 0.471$), and aluminum ($\beta = 0.379$, $r = 0.451$) (Figure 1b–e), and these mean burden levels in infants/children were significantly higher than those in their mothers (Table 1).

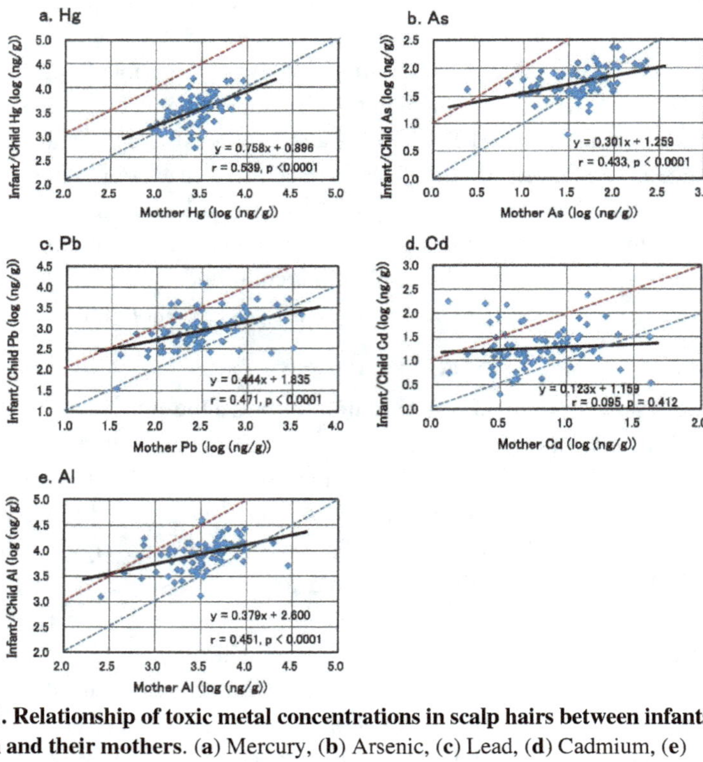

Figure 1. Relationship of toxic metal concentrations in scalp hairs between infants/ children and their mothers. (**a**) Mercury, (**b**) Arsenic, (**c**) Lead, (**d**) Cadmium, (**e**) Aluminum. Dotted blue line and red line represent the toxic metal concentrations in

infants/children equal to and 10 times higher than those in their mothers, respectively.

In particular, for lead, cadmium and aluminum, these mean burden levels in infants/children were approximately three times higher than those in their mothers, and the burden levels in some individuals exhibited several tens of times higher than those in their mothers. Namely the maximum values for lead, cadmium, and aluminum in infants/children were 11,930 (1-year-old girl), 241 (2-year-old boy) and 40,740 ng/g (2-year-old boy), which was 35, 41, and 12 times higher than mean levels in the mothers, respectively (Table 1).

Table 1. Mean toxic metal concentrations in scalp hairs of infant/child and their mothers

Toxic Metal	Geometric Mean (ng/g)		Maximum in Infant/Child		
	Mother	Infant/Child			
	(N = 77)	(N = 77)	(ng/g)	Ratio	
Hg	2,621	3,057	15,140	5.8	(F 5)
As	41.2	55.5	233	5.7	(M4)
Pb	338	907	11,930	35.3	(F 1)
Cd	5.9	17.9	241	40.8	(M2)
Al	3,362	8,645	40,740	12.1	(M2)

Statistically significant difference in the mean value in infant/child group compared to their mother group is shown with asterisk marks: * $p < 0.05$, **** $p < 0.0001$. Maximum value for each toxic metal concentration in infant/child and ratio to mother is shown. Alphabet (M, F) and numeral in parentheses represent gender (male, female) and age of the subject who showed maximum value for each metal.

Infants/children were divided into three groups by age; 0-3, 4-9, and 10-11 years-old, and mean concentrations of the five toxic metals in each group were calculated and compared to their mothers (Figure 2). The mean burden levels of lead, cadmium, and aluminum in infant group of 0-3 year-olds were highest, high-significantly different from their mothers ($p < 0.0001$) and declined with age (Figure 2c–e), while such an age-dependency was not observed in those of mercury and arsenic (Figure 2a,b).

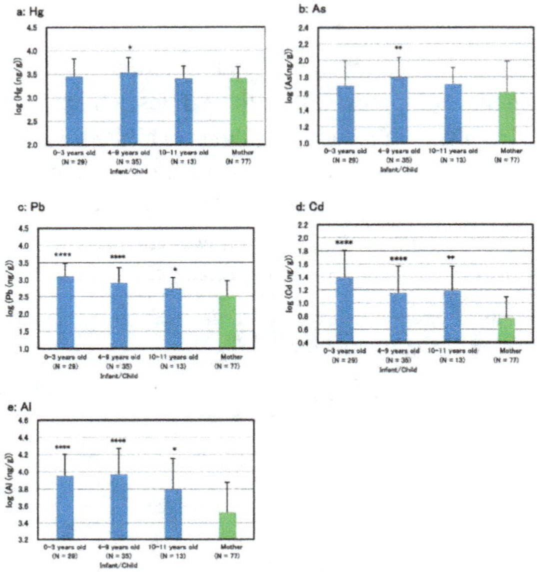

Figure 2. Geometric mean toxic metal concentrations in infants/children grouped by age and their mothers. (**a**) Mercury, (**b**) Arsenic, (**c**) Lead, (**d**) Cadmium, (**e**) Aluminum. Infants/children were grouped by age; 0–3, 4–9, and 10–11 year-old, and the geometric mean concentrations of toxic metals in each group were compared to those in their mothers. Statistically significant difference in the mean value in each age-group compared to their mother group is shown with asterisk marks: * $p < 0.05$, ** $p < 0.01$, **** $p < 0.0001$.

Among essential minerals, the levels of some elements, such as chromium, molybdenum, manganese, iron, and iodine in infants/children were significantly nearly two times higher than those in their mothers as well as for the above toxic metals. In contrast, the limited three elements of zinc, magnesium and calcium in infants/children were significantly lower than those in their mothers ($p < 0.0001$) (Table 2), and 29, 9 and 8 individuals (37.7, 11.7 and 10.4 %) in the infants/children group were estimated to be zinc-, magnesium- and calcium-deficient, respectively. There were a few or no individuals with deficiency in iron, copper, manganese, chromium, and molybdenum.

Table 2. Mean essential mineral concentrations in scalp hairs of infant/child and their mother.

Essential	Geometric Mean (ng/g)			Deficient Infant/Child	
Mineral	Mother	Infant/Child	Significance	Cases	Rate
	(N = 77)	(N = 77)			(%)
Na	16,804	13,307	NS		
K	10,542	17,976	**		
Mg	76,513	27,929	****	9	11.7
Ca	710,404	294,933	****	8	10.4
P	117,833	102,574	NS		
Se	587	577	NS	0	0
I	196	404	***	0	0
Cr	34.9	74.1	****	2	2.6
Mo	33.1	59.1	****	0	0
Mn	108	174	***	0	0
Fe	4,514	7,922	****	1	1.3
Cu	22,967	19,175	NS	0	0
Zn	135,620	97,139	****	29	37.7

Statistically significant difference in mean concentrations in infant/child group compared to their mother group is shown with asterisk marks: ** $p < 0.01$, *** $p < 0.001$, **** $p < 0.0001$.

The mutual relationship of these toxic metals and essential minerals were examined by multiple regression analysis, and the correlation coefficients between some metal-metal combinations are shown in Table 3. In infants/children, statistically significant positive correlations were observed between cadmium and lead ($r = 0.616$, $p < 0.0001$), aluminum and lead ($r = 0.347$, $p = 0.002$), and aluminum and iron ($r = 0.601$, $p < 0.0001$). In their mothers, similar positive relationships were observed in each metal-metal combination ($r = 0.438$, $p < 0.0001$; $r = 0.273$, $p = 0.016$; $r = 0.426$, $p = 0.0001$, respectively). About iron element, not only these toxic metals but also various metals such as manganese, cobalt, chromium, molybdenum, and nickel so on positively correlate with iron (data not shown), suggesting co-burdens of iron with a variety of heavy metals.

In contrast, statistically significant inverse correlations were observed between zinc and lead ($r = -0.267$, $p = 0.019$), between magnesium and arsenic ($r = -0.514$, $p < 0.0001$) and between zinc and molybdenum ($r = -0.331$, $p = 0.003$) in infants/children, and in mothers between magnesium and arsenic ($r = -0.649$, $p < 0.0001$). It is emphasized that zinc element is only one heavy essential metal exhibiting inverse relationship between various heavy metals, as previously reported [4,5,20]. Among minerals, the highest positive correlation is observed between calcium and magnesium in both the infant/child and mother group ($r = 0.871$ and 0.820, respectively, $p < 0.0001$).

Table 3. Relationship of metal-metal pair concentrations in infants/children and in their mothers.

Metal-Metal Correlation	Infant/Child (N = 77) Coefficient	p-Value		Mother (N = 77) Coefficient	p-Value	
Cd-Pb	0.616	0.000	****	0.438	0.000	****
Al-Pb	0.347	0.002	**	0.273	0.016	*
Al-Fe	0.601	0.000	****	0.426	0.001	***
Pb-Zn	-0.267	0.019	*	0.139	0.227	
As-Mg	-0.514	0.000	****	-0.649	0.000	****
Zn-Mo	-0.331	0.003	**	-0.183	0.112	
Ca-Mg	0.871	0.000	****	0.820	0.000	****

Statistically significant correlation is shown by p-value and asterisk marks: * $p < 0.05$, ** $p < 0.01$, *** $p < 0.001$, **** $p < 0.0001$.

Representative metallome profiles of four individuals with high burdens of some toxic metals and/or with deficiency in essential metals are shown in Figure 3, together with those of their mothers.

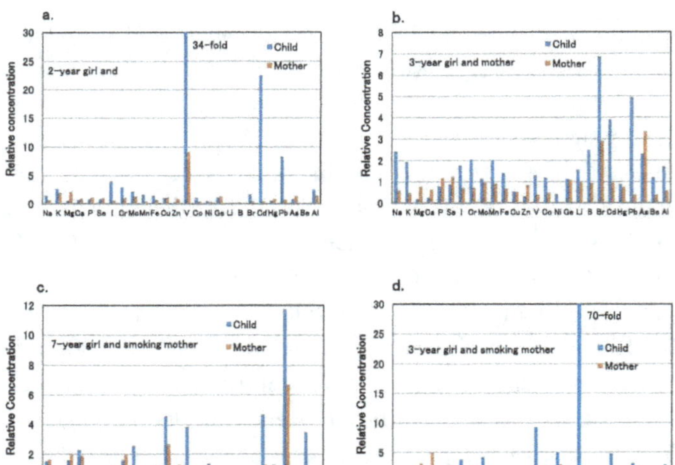

Figure 3. Metallome profiles of four child/mother pairs with some toxic metal burdens and/or essential metal deficiency. Each bar (blue and red) represents the relative concentration of the respective trace element in child's and the mother's scalp hair specimens, respectively. The 1.0 of the relative concentration represents the reference control level of each trace element. (**a**) A typical metallome profile of a 2-year-old girl and her mother is shown, exhibiting severe zinc deficiency and simultaneous high burdens with vanadium, cadmium, and lead in the child. (**b**) Another typical metallome profile of a 3-year-old girl and her mother is shown, exhibiting severe magnesium deficiency and simultaneous burdens with lead, cadmium, and bromine in the child. (**c**) A typical metallome profile of a 7-year-old girl and her smoking mother is shown, exhibiting severe lead burden and simultaneous burdens with cadmium,

copper, and vanadium in the child. (**d**) Another typical metallome profile of a 3-year-old girl and her smoking mother is shown, exhibiting sever lithium burden and simultaneous burdens with vanadium, nickel, and cadmium in the child.

The first (Figure 3a) and second (Figure 3b) cases showed a marked zinc deficiency with high burdens of cadmium and lead, while concentrations of these three metals in the mothers were almost normal levels. In the first case, a marked high burden of vanadium was also observed, and its burden level was nearly four times higher than that of her mother. The third and fourth cases, whose mother had a habit of smoking, showed high accumulation of not only cadmium and lead, but also vanadium, copper or lithium than the respective mother, while zinc levels were normal (Figure 3c and d).

Discussion

The pathogenic roles of some toxic metals such as mercury, lead, aluminum, or cadmium have been interested in various neurodegenerative diseases [1–3,8–10]. These toxic metals are also known to cause some fraction of neurodevelopmental disabilities [4–7,14]. Gardner et al. [11] reported that early-life cadmium exposure had the strongest and most consistent inverse association with children's growth in terms of weight and height. Choi et al. [12] demonstrated that post-birth weight gain was negatively associated with blood levels of lead, and similar negative association for current head circumference with arsenic and lead.

In this study, the geometric mean concentration of mercury in infants/children was of similar level to that in their mothers (Table 1), and statistically high-significant close correlation between mothers and infants/children was observed (Figure 1a), suggesting equivalent exposure to mercury in infants/children and mothers due to their common lifestyles. A significant but less intimate mother/child relationship was observed for arsenic, lead and aluminum (Figure 1b–e), and the proportion of infants/children with higher burdens than mother was larger than that of mercury, and these mean burden levels in infants/children were significantly higher than those in their mothers (Table 1). Remarkably, the mean burden levels of lead, cadmium and aluminum in infants/children were found to be approximately three times higher than those in their mothers, the differences being statistically high-significant (Table 1). The burden levels of these three toxic metals in some infants/children were several tens of times higher than those in mothers (Figure 1c–e). It should be noted that the burden levels of lead, cadmium and aluminum in mothers, whose infants/children showed maximal or sub-maximal levels, were not so high. These findings indicate that these three toxic metals are liable to accumulate in infants/children more than in their mothers.

The burden levels of lead, cadmium, and aluminum in infants of 0-3 years-old were highest and declined with age inversely, while such an inverse age-dependency was not observed in those of mercury and arsenic (Figure 2). These results are coincident with our previous study, suggesting that the three toxic metals of lead, cadmium and aluminum are characteristic liable to accumulate in infants and different from mercury and arsenic which have a character accumulating in adults age-dependently [3]. In addition, statistically significant positive correlations were observed between cadmium and lead, and between aluminum and lead in both infants/children and mothers (Table 3), suggesting that the mechanisms of distribution, detoxification, and excretion of these three toxic metals are different from those of mercury and arsenic. High close correlation between aluminum and iron in infants/children (Table 3) seems to suggest multiple pollutions with some related-metals such as manganese and chromium, as shown in Table 2.

In contrast to toxic metals, the mean concentrations of magnesium, calcium and zinc in infants/children were significantly lower than those in their mothers, and 29 and 9 individuals (37.7 and 11.7%) in the 77 child subjects were estimated to be zinc- and magnesium-deficient, respectively (Table 2). In addition, statistically significant inverse correlations were observed between concentrations of zinc and lead, and between magnesium and arsenic in infants/children (Table 3). A significant inverse correlation between magnesium and arsenic was also observed in their mothers, but not between zinc and lead, suggesting characteristic interaction between zinc and lead in infants/children [4,5,14]. No significant correlation between zinc and cadmium or between zinc and aluminum was observed in this study, but our previous study for larger number of autistic children has revealed high burdens of lead, cadmium and aluminum accompanied by deficiency in zinc and magnesium, and significant relationships between these toxic metal burdens and zinc deficiency [3–5,14,20]. It is, therefore, speculated that the relative and absolute deficiency in antagonistic metals such as zinc and magnesium are associated with the accumulation of toxic metals, as observed in this study.

In fact, dietary restriction-induced zinc deficiency has been reported to up-regulate intestinal zinc-importer (Zip4) and induce the increase in Zip4 protein located to the plasma membrane of enterocytes [21–24]. This adaptive response to zinc deficiency is known to induce increasing in the risk of high uptake of toxic metals such as cadmium and lead [25]. Thus, infants with zinc deficiency are liable to be exposed to increased risk of absorbing high amounts of toxic metals and retaining them in their body. In addition, maternal cigarette smoking was reported to be associated with lower zinc and higher cadmium and lead concentrations in their neonates [26]. Because of their high distribution property to bone tissue, during pregnancy and lactation, these toxic metals accumulated in the maternal bone matrix are co-transferred with calcium and magnesium to fetal and newborn bodies through increased bone-resorption [27,28].

As shown in Figure 1, toxic metal burden levels in infants appear to be affected profoundly by those in their mothers through placental transfer during pregnancy and breastfeeding after birth, which are affected by foods/drinks, smoking, or passive smoking and other environmental factors. High contents of toxic metals (cadmium, lead and aluminum) in tobacco and high exposure to these toxic metals in smokers and their family members have been reported [29–32]. Toxic metal burdens in infants are also affected by infant formulas or weaning foods: higher concentration of cadmium in soy-based and cereal-based formulas than cow's milk formulas and high content of aluminum in infant formulas and vaccine preparations have been reported [33–37].

It is known that breast-fed infants are prone to develop trace element deficiency and that alopecia and dermatitis are attributable to zinc deficiency. Furthermore, "follow-up milk" formulas (nutritional supplement for infants aged over 6-month) used in Japan contain practically iron and calcium fortified but neither zinc nor copper, and the dependence on the follow-up milk formulas as the main source of nutrition is reported to be associated with a high risk of zinc deficiency [38].

Recently, Fiore et al. [8] reported that there was a negative, significant association between hair zinc level and severity of autistic symptoms (defective functional play and creativity and increase of stereotyped behavior), and lead, molybdenum and manganese hair levels were inversely correlated with cognitive level (full intelligence quotient) in autism spectrum disorder (ASD) individuals.

Thus, it is suggested that supplementation of deficient essential metals such as zinc and magnesium in early period of infant/child is expected to ameliorate the body metal imbalances and probably the clinical symptoms related to their deficiencies and toxic metal burdens in the early neurodevelopment period, named "Infantile Time Window" or "First 1000 Days" [4,5,13–15,19,39,40].

Arnold et al. [41] reported that mean serum zinc levels were significantly lower in both autism and attention deficit/hyperactivity disorder (ADHD) groups, and that serum zinc level correlated inversely with parent- and teacher-rated inattention in ADHD children. Furthermore, it is reported that zinc supplementation reduces symptoms of hyperactivity, impulsivity, and impaired socialization in ADHD patients [42,43]. Other preliminary human study showed that zinc supplement as an adjunct to methylphenidate has favorable effects in the treatment of ADHD children [44]. The critical role of zinc deficiency in etiology of ASD has been suggested by recent studies showing high uptake of neurotoxin lead and reduced uptake of essential minerals manganese and zinc during specific developmental windows [4–6] and disruption of zinc-copper rhythmicity [7] in those children. Furthermore, it has been suggested that zinc signaling through Shank2 and Shank3 controls the AMPA receptor subunit switch in developing neurons, and that zinc deficiency may impair synaptic maturation and circuit formation that underlie ASD etiology [17–19]. Recently, Miyake et al. [45] found the association between maternal smoking and DNA hypo-methylation of zinc-dependent Shank2 synaptic scaffolding gene in cord blood, suggesting the epigenetic and unfavorable effect of smoking on neurodevelopment in infants and fetus.

Kozielec et al. [46] reported that in hyperactive children with ADHD, magnesium deficiency was found in the 95% of the subjects and reported that a significant decrease of hyperactivity and increase in hair magnesium contents has been achieved in the group of ADHD children given six months of magnesium supplementation [47]. Mousain-Bosc et al. [48] also reported that 52 hyper-excitable children have low intra-erythrocyte magnesium levels with normal serum magnesium values and that magnesium/vitamin B6 supplementation can restore the erythrocyte magnesium levels to normal and improve their abnormal behaviors. They also reported that 33 children with clinical symptoms of pervasive developmental disorder (PDD) or autism exhibit significantly lower red blood cell magnesium values and that the combination therapy with magnesium/vitamin B6 for six months improved significantly PDD symptoms with concomitant increases in intra-erythrocyte magnesium values [49].

Such an evidence-based nutritional approach supplementing deficient nutrients and detoxifying accumulated toxic metals is of great importance for normal growth and development of infants and children, and probably yields a new pathway into prevention and treatment of neurodevelopment disorders such as ASD, ADHD and also learning disorders [4,5,13,19,50].

The present study was cross-sectional, and detailed information about health conditions, dietary habits and environmental factors of the subjects was lacking. Nevertheless, a careful assessment and monitoring of such infants and children suffered from some essential metal deficiencies and/or toxic metal burdens revealed in this study would be essential, and if necessary, supplementing deficient metals should be considered. Therefore, it is expected that larger epidemiological and intervention studies will clarify the pathogenic relationship between infantile metal imbalances described above and neurodevelopment disorders, and thereby provide reasonable and essential procedures for their normal growth and neurodevelopment. In addition, clinical metallomics (or "mineralomics") analysis with another micronutrient omics "vitaminomics" analysis will be used as an essential tool for personalized precision medicine in the near future.

Conclusions

In this cross-sectional study of 77 pairs of Japanese infants/children and their mothers, a high-significant close child/mother relationship was demonstrated for mercury burden levels. For the other toxic metals such as lead, cadmium and aluminum, these burden levels in children, particularly in infants, were markedly higher than those in their mothers, with less intimate child/mother relationship. In contrast, the levels of zinc, magnesium, and calcium, which can compete against and antagonize toxic metals, were found to be significantly low in infants/children. High burdens of toxic metals and deficiencies of antagonistic essential metals in infants/children are of serious concern, and early assessment and intervention for such subjects would be helpful for their normal growth and development.

Author Contributions: H.Y. planned this study, analyzed the data and wrote the manuscript, with the help of T.T. and K.S. All authors have read and agree to the published version of the manuscript.

Funding: This research perceived no external funding.

Institutional Review Board Statement: This study was conducted according to the guidelines of the Declaration of Helsinki, and approved by the Institutional Review Board.

Informed Consent Statement: Informed consent was obtained from all subjects involved in the study.

Acknowledgments: The authors sincerely appreciate the mother/child pair subjects for their cooperation. They thank the laboratory team for their technical contributions to hair mineral analysis and O. Shimada for his help.

Conflicts of Interest: The authors declare no competing financial interests.

References

1. Harada, M. Minamata Disease: Methylmercury Poisoning in Japan Caused by Environmental Pollution. *Crit. Rev. Toxicol.* **1995**, *25*, 1–24. [CrossRef] [PubMed]

2. Silbergeld, E.K. Preventing lead poisoning in children. *Annu. Rev. Public Health* **1997**, *18*, 187–210. [CrossRef] [PubMed]

3. Yasuda, H.; Yoshida, K.; Yasuda, Y.; Tsutsui, T. Two age-related accumulation profiles of toxic metals. *Curr. Aging Sci.* **2012**, *5*, 105–111. [CrossRef] [PubMed]

4. Yasuda, H.; Yasuda, Y.; Tsutsui, T. Estimation of autistic children by

metallomics analysis. *Sci. Rep.* **2013**, *3*, srep01199. [CrossRef]
5. Yasuda, H.; Tsutsui, T. Assessment of Infantile Mineral Imbalances in Autism Spectrum Disorders (ASDs). *Int. J. Environ. Res. Public Health* **2013**, *10*, 6027–6043. [CrossRef]
6. Arora, M.; Reichenberg, A.; Willfors, C.; Austin, C.; Gennings, C.; Berggren, S.; Lichtenstein, P.; Anckarsäter, H.; Tammimies, K.; Bölte, S. Fetal and postnatal metal dysregulation in autism. *Nat. Commun.* **2017**, *8*, 15493. [CrossRef]
7. Curtin, P.; Austin, C.; Curtin, A.; Gennings, C.; Arora, M.; Tammimies, K.; Willfors, C.; Berggren, S.; Siper, P.; Rai, D.; et al. Dynamical features in fetal and postnatal zinc-copper metabolic cycles predict the emergence of autism spectrum disorder. *Sci. Adv.* **2018**, *4*, eaat1293. [CrossRef]
8. Fiore, M.; Barone, R.; Copat, C.; Grasso, A.; Cristaldi, A.; Rizzo, R.; Ferrante, M. Metal and essential element levels in hair and association with autism severity. *J. Trace Elements Med. Biol.* **2020**, *57*, 126409. [CrossRef]
9. Cicero, C.E.; Mostile, G.; Vasta, R.; Rapisarda, V.; Signorelli, S.S.; Ferrante, M.; Zappia, M.; Nicoletti, A. Metals and neurodegener- ative diseases. A systematic review. *Environ. Res.* **2017**, *159*, 82–94. [CrossRef]
10. McLachlan, D.R.C.; Bergeron, C.; Alexandrov, P.N.; Walsh, W.J.; Pogue, A.I.; Percy, M.E.; Kruck, T.P.A.; Fang, Z.; Sharfman, N.M.; Jaber, V.; et al. Retraction Note: Aluminum in Neurological and Neurodegenerative Disease. *Mol. Neurobiol.* **2020**, *57*, 1779. [CrossRef]
11. Gardner, R.M.; Kippler, M.; Tofail, F.; Bottai, M.; Hamadani, J.D.; Grandér, M.; Nermell, B.; Palm, B.; Rasmussen, K.M.; Vahter, M. Environmental Exposure to Metals and Children's Growth to Age 5 Years: A Prospective Cohort Study. *Am. J. Epidemiology* **2013**, *177*, 1356–1367. [CrossRef] [PubMed]
12. Choi, J.; Chang, J.Y.; Hong, J.; Shin, S.; Park, J.S.; Oh, S. Low-Level Toxic Metal Exposure in Healthy Weaning-Age Infants: Association with Growth, Dietary Intake, and Iron Deficiency. *Int. J. Environ. Res. Public Health* **2017**, *14*, 388. [CrossRef] [PubMed]
13. Yasuda, H.; Yoshida, K.; Yasuda, Y.; Tsutsui, T. Infantile zinc deficiency: Association with autism spectrum disorders. *Sci. Rep.* **2011**, *1*, 129. [CrossRef] [PubMed]
14. Yasuda, H. Early assessment and intervention of mineral imbalances for autistic children. In *Autism Spectrum Disorders*; Valdez, A., Ed.; Nova Science Publishers: New York, NY, USA, 2013; pp. 27–49.
15. Cusick, S.E.; Georgieff, M.K. The Role of Nutrition in Brain Development: The Golden Opportunity of the "First 1000 Days". *J. Pediatr.* **2016**, *175*, 16–21. [CrossRef]
16. Austin, C.; Curtin, P.; Curtin, A.; Gennings, C.; Arora, M.; Tammimies, K.;

Isaksson, J.; Willfors, C.; Bölte, S. Dynamical properties of elemental metabolism distinguish attention deficit hyperactivity disorder from autism spectrum disorder. *Transl. Psychiatry* **2019**, *9*, 1–9. [CrossRef]

17. Pfaender, S.; Sauer, A.K.; Hagmeyer, S.; Mangus, K.; Linta, L.; Liebau, S.; Bockmann, J.; Huguet, G.; Bourgeron, T.; Boeckers, T.M.; et al. Zinc deficiency and low enterocyte zinc transporter expression in human patients with autism related mutations in SHANK3. *Sci. Rep.* **2017**, *7*, 45190. [CrossRef]

18. Ha, H.T.T.; Leal-Ortiz, S.; Lalwani, K.; Kiyonaka, S.; Hamachi, I.; Mysore, S.P.; Montgomery, J.M.; Garner, C.C.; Huguenard, J.R.; Kim, S.A. Shank and Zinc Mediate an AMPA Receptor Subunit Switch in Developing Neurons. *Front. Mol. Neurosci.* **2018**, *11*, 405. [CrossRef]

19. Hagmeyer, S.; Sauer, A.K.; Grabrucker, A.M. Prospects of Zinc Supplementation in Autism Spectrum Disorders and Shankopathies Such as Phelan McDermid Syndrome. *Front. Synaptic Neurosci.* **2018**, *10*, 11. [CrossRef]

20. Yasuda, H.; Tsutsui, T. Infants and elderlies are susceptible to zinc deficiency. *Sci. Rep.* **2016**, *6*, 21850. [CrossRef]

21. Dufner-Beattie, J.; Wang, F.; Kuo, Y.-M.; Gitschier, J.; Eide, D.; Andrews, G.K. The Acrodermatitis Enteropathica Gene ZIP4 Encodes a Tissue-specific, Zinc-regulated Zinc Transporter in Mice. *J. Biol. Chem.* **2003**, *278*, 33474–33481. [CrossRef]

22. Dufner-Beattie, J.; Kuo, Y.-M.; Gitschier, J.; Andrews, G.K. The Adaptive Response to Dietary Zinc in Mice Involves the Differential Cellular Localization and Zinc Regulation of the Zinc Transporters ZIP4 and ZIP5. *J. Biol. Chem.* **2004**, *279*, 49082–49090. [CrossRef] [PubMed]

23. Cousins, R.J.; Liuzzi, J.P.; Lichten, L.A. Mammalian Zinc Transport, Trafficking, and Signals. *J. Biol. Chem.* **2006**, *281*, 24085–24089. [CrossRef]

24. Lichten, L.A.; Cousins, R.J. Mammalian Zinc Transporters: Nutritional and Physiologic Regulation. *Annu. Rev. Nutr.* **2009**, *29*, 153–176. [CrossRef] [PubMed]

25. Goyer, R.A. Toxic and essential metal interactions. *Annu. Rev. Nutr.* **1997**, *17*, 37–50. [CrossRef] [PubMed]

26. Razagui, I.B.-A.; Ghribi, I. Maternal and Neonatal Scalp Hair Concentrations of Zinc, Copper, Cadmium, and Lead: Relationship to Some Lifestyle Factors. *Biol. Trace Element Res.* **2005**, *106*, 001–028. [CrossRef]

27. Symanski, E.; Hertz-Picciotto, I. Blood Lead Levels in Relation to Menopause, Smoking, and Pregnancy History. *Am. J. Epidemiol.* **1995**, *141*, 1047–1058. [CrossRef]

28. Gulson, B.; Jameson, C.; Mahaffey, K.; Mizon, K.; Korsch, M.; Vimpani, G. Pregnancy increases mobilization of lead from maternal skeleton. *J. Lab. Clin.*

Med. **1997**, *130*, 51–62. [CrossRef]

29. Exley, C.; Begum, A.; Woolley, M.P.; Bloor, R.N. Aluminum in Tobacco and Cannabis and Smoking-Related Disease. *Am. J. Med.* **2006**, *119*, 276.e9–276.e11. [CrossRef]

30. Mutti, A.; Corradi, M.; Goldoni, M.; Vettori, M.V.; Bernard, A.; Apostoli, P. Exhaled Metallic Elements and Serum Pneumoproteins in Asymptomatic Smokers and Patients with COPD or Asthma. *Chest* **2006**, *129*, 1288–1297. [CrossRef]

31. Serdar, M.; Akin, B.S.; Razi, C.; Akin, O.; Tokgoz, S.; Kenar, L.; Aykut, O. The Correlation between Smoking Status of Family Members and Concentrations of Toxic Trace Elements in the Hair of Children. *Biol. Trace Element Res.* **2012**, *148*, 11–17. [CrossRef]

32. Unkiewicz-Winiarczyk, A.; Gromysz-Kałkowska, K.; Szubartowska, E. Aluminium, Cadmium and Lead Concentration in the Hair of Tobacco Smokers. *Biol. Trace Element Res.* **2009**, *132*, 41–50. [CrossRef] [PubMed]

33. Eklund, G.; Oskarsson, A. Exposure of cadmium from infant formulas and weaning foods. *Food Addit. Contam.* **1999**, *16*, 509–519. [CrossRef]

34. Freundlich, M.; Abitbol, C.; Zilleruelo, G.; Strauss, J.; Faugere, M.-C.; Malluche, H. Infant formula as a cause of Aluminium toxicity in neonatal URAEMIA. *Lancet* **1985**, *326*, 527–529. [CrossRef]

35. Fernandez-Lorenzo, J.R.; Cocho, J.A.; Rey-Goldar, M.L.; Couce, M.; Fraga, J.M. Aluminum Contents of Human Milk, Cow's Milk, and Infant Formulas. *J. Pediatr. Gastroenterol. Nutr.* **1999**, *28*, 270–275. [CrossRef] [PubMed]

36. Lyons-Weiler, J.; Ricketson, R. Reconsideration of the immunotherapeutic pediatric safe dose levels of aluminum. *J. Trace Elements Med. Biol.* **2018**, *48*, 67–73. [CrossRef]

37. Exley, C. An aluminium adjuvant in a vaccine is an acute exposure to aluminium. *J. Trace Elements Med. Biol.* **2020**, *57*, 57–59. [CrossRef]

38. Kodama, H. Trace Element Deficiency in Infants and Children: Clinical Practice. *Jpn. Med. Assoc. J.* **2004**, *47*, 376–381.

39. Bölte, S.; Girdler, S.; Marschik, P.B. The contribution of environmental exposure to the etiology of autism spectrum disorder. *Cell. Mol. Life Sci.* **2019**, *76*, 1275–1297. [CrossRef]

40. Masini, E.; Loi, E.; Vega-Benedetti, A.F.; Carta, M.; Doneddu, G.; Fadda, R.; Zavattari, P. An Overview of the Main Genetic, Epigenetic and Environmental Factors Involved in Autism Spectrum Disorder Focusing on Synaptic Activity. *Int. J. Mol. Sci.* **2020**, *21*, 8290. [CrossRef]

41. Arnold, L.E.; Bozzolo, H.; Hollway, J.; Cook, A.; DiSilvestro, R.A.; Bozzolo, D.R.; Crowl, L.; Ramadan, Y.; Williams, C. Serum Zinc Correlates with Parent-

and Teacher-Rated Inattention in Children with Attention-Deficit/Hyperactivity Disorder. *J. Child Adolesc. Psychopharmacol.* **2005**, *15*, 628–636. [CrossRef]

42. Yorbik, O.; Ozdag, M.F.; Olgun, A.; Senol, M.G.; Bek, S.; Akman, S. Potential effects of zinc on information processing in boys with attention deficit hyperactivity disorder. *Prog. Neuro-Psychopharmacol. Biol. Psychiatry* **2008**, *32*, 662–667. [CrossRef] [PubMed]

43. DiGirolamo, A.M.; Ramirez-Zea, M.; Wang, M.; Flores-Ayala, R.; Martorell, R.; Neufeld, L.M.; Ramakrishnan, U.; Sellen, D.; Black, M.M.; Stein, A.D. Randomized trial of the effect of zinc supplementation on the mental health of school-age children in Guatemala. *Am. J. Clin. Nutr.* **2010**, *92*, 1241–1250. [CrossRef] [PubMed]

44. Akhondzadeh, S.; Mohammadi, M.R.; Khademi, M. Zinc sulfate as an adjunct to methylphenidate for the treatment of attention deficit hyperactivity disorder in children: A double blind and randomized trial [ISRCTN64132371]. *BMC Psychiatry* **2004**, *4*, 9. [CrossRef] [PubMed]

45. Miyake, K.; Kawaguchi, A.; Miura, R.; Kobayashi, S.; Tran, N.Q.V.; Kobayashi, S.; Miyashita, C.; Araki, A.; Kubota, T.; Yamagata, Z.; et al. Association between DNA methylation in cord blood and maternal smoking: The Hokkaido Study on Environment and Children's Health. *Sci. Rep.* **2018**, *8*, 5654. [CrossRef]

46. Kozielec, T.; Starobrat-Hermelin, B. Assessment of magnesium levels in children with attention deficit hyperactivity disorder (ADHD). *Magnes. Res.* **1997**, *10*, 143–148.

47. Starobrat-Hermelin, B.; Kozielec, T. The effects of magnesium physiological supplementation on hyperactivity in children with attention deficit hyperactivity disorder (ADHD). Positive response to magnesium oral loading test. *Magnes. Res.* **1997**, *10*, 149–156.

48. Mousain-Bosc, M.; Roche, M.; Rapin, J.; Bali, J.-P. Magnesium VitB6 Intake Reduces Central Nervous System Hyperexcitability in Children. *J. Am. Coll. Nutr.* **2004**, *23*, 545S–548S. [CrossRef]

49. Mousain-Bosc, M.; Roche, M.; Polge, A.; Pradal-Prat, D.; Rapin, J.; Bali, J. Improvement of neurobehavioral disorders in children supplemented with magnesium-vitamin B6. II. Pervasive developmental disorder-autism. *Magnes. Res.* **2006**, *19*, 53–62.

50. Botturi, A.; Ciappolino, V.; DelVecchio, G.; Boscutti, A.; Viscardi, B.; Brambilla, P. The Role and the Effect of Magnesium in Mental Disorders: A Systematic Review. *Nutrients* **2020**, *12*, 1661. [CrossRef]

Chapter 5:

METALLOMICS ANALYSIS FOR EARLY ASSESSMENT AND INDIVIDUALIZED INTERVENTION OF NEURODEVELOPMENTAL DISORDERS

published in **Metallomics 11: mfac067 (2022).**

Hiroshi Yasuda and **Toyoharu Tsutsui**
La Belle Vie Research Laboratory, Chuo-ku, Tokyo, Japan

Abstract

The children today are in the midst of the epidemic of neurodevelopmental disorders. In this metallomics study for the scalp hair samples of total 2550 children with autistic disorders (2108 males and 442 females aged 0-15 years), it was demonstrated that near one-half of the infantile individuals aged 0-3 years are suffering from zinc deficiency and toxic metal burdens. Zinc level correlated closely to the index of zinc/iron ratio more than zinc/copper ratio. Furthermore, there were significant relationships between zinc deficiency and toxic metal burdens such as lead and aluminum, which were inversely associated with not only zinc level but also zinc/iron ratio with higher regression coefficients of r = -0.486 and -0.551 ($p < 0.00001$), respectively. High-significant inverse association was detected between zinc and molybdenum concentration (r = -0.509) and also between zinc/iron ratio and molybdenum (r = -0.548). These findings suggest that infantile zinc deficiency relates to the high burdens of not only toxic but also some essential metals such as molybdenum, iron, and manganese and that these various mineral imbalances play principal roles in the etiology of neurodevelopmental disorders. We expect that the early assessment and intervention of the mineral imbalances (dis-homeostasis) in individual child open an avenue for evidence-based individualized treatment of neurodevelopmental disorders and also of the comorbid immune disorders, in near future.

Keywords: metallomics analysis, neurodevelopmental disorders, zinc deficiency, toxic metal burdens, mineral imbalances, zinc/iron ratio, infantile time window, individualized intervention

Graphical abstract

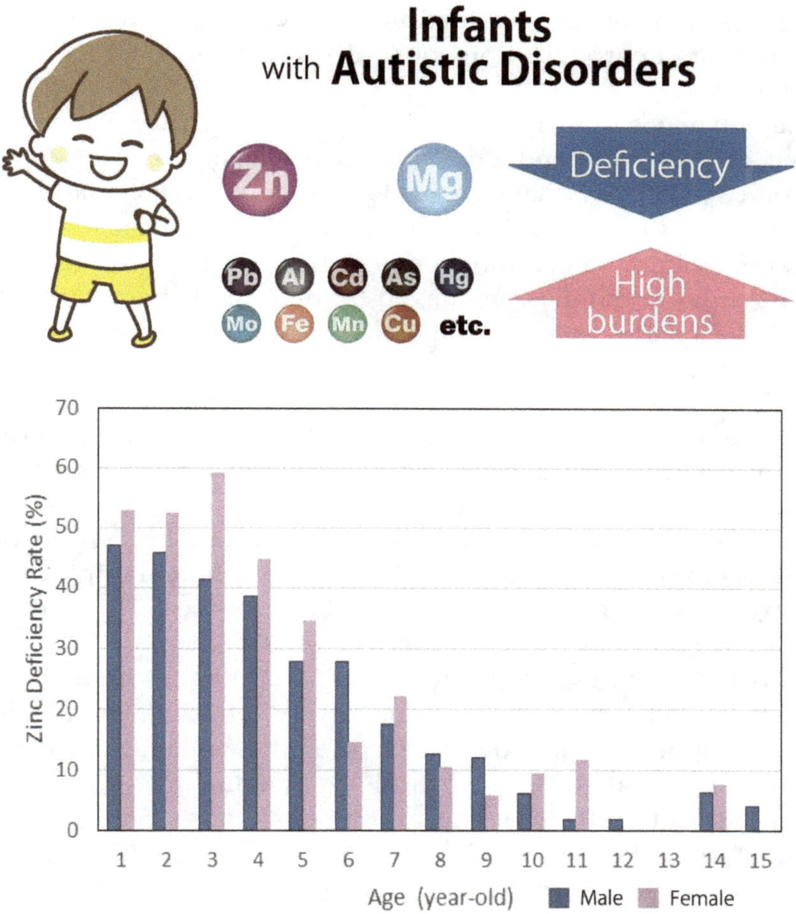

Infantile Zn and Mg deficiency and high burdens of toxic metals

Introduction

The children today in developed countries are in the midst of the epidemic of neurodevelopmental disorders such as autism spectrum disorder (ASD) and attention-deficit/hyperactivity disorder (ADHD). These disorders are a group of neurodevelopmental disorders heritable with a strong genetic basis of 65 or more candidate genes, and their prevalence has been increasing to 13%.[1-4] However, the key genetic determinants are still unclarified and the interaction of hereditary factors with some environmental factors seems play a critical role in the pathogenesis.[3] Thus, the elucidation of the etiology and effective treatment of neurodevelopmental disorders is one of the challenges today.

Great advances in a high-sensitive and reliable trace element analysis method using inductively coupled plasma mass spectrometry (ICP-MS) have enabled us to apply it to medical research and estimate the chronic toxic metal burden and mineral deficiency in the human body.[5-7]

In the previous studies, we have reported that some restricted mineral deficiency (e.g. zinc and magnesium) and toxic metal burdens, especially during the restricted time window of 0-3 year old, epigenetically play principal roles as environmental factors in autistic disorders and that metallomics approach lead to early screening and prevention of the neurodevelopmental disorders.[6–9]

This infantile zinc-deficiency-related epigenetic hypothesis of neurodevelopmental disorders has been supported and reinforced by many research groups[10-17] and has been expected to lead to approaching its early intervention/treatment.[9,17-20]

In this metallomics study for total 2550 children with autistic disorders, it is demonstrated that many children with the neurodevelopmental disorders are suffered from high burdens of some essential metals such as molybdenum, iron, and manganese, not only toxic metal burdens. Furthermore, it is suggested that the index of zinc/iron ratio is another useful biomarker for assessment of the Japanese children suffered from neurodevelopmental disorders. We expect that the early assessment and intervention of various mineral imbalances open an avenue for evidence-based individualized therapy for neurodevelopmental disorders and also their comorbid allergic immune disorders.

Materials and methods

Samples and trace element analysis

Human scalp hair, a kind of cellular body, is widely used as a non-invasive, stable, and useful biospecimen for assessment of environmental exposure of toxic metals, for evaluation of nutritional status, and in forensic science.[5,7,8,16,20]

On the basis of informed consent, scalp hair samples from 2550 (male: 2108; female: 442) autistic Japanese subjects aged 0-15 years were collected in the period from June 2005 to September 2015, although 0-year-old subject was only two (10- and 11-month-old female). These subjects were comprised of the children diagnosed with ASD by their physicians. Hair sampling was recommended to cut as close to the scalp of the occipital area as possible.

Hair sample of 75 mg was weighed into a 50 ml plastic tube and washed with acetone and then with a 0.01% triton solution, as recommended by the Hair Analysis Standardization Board. The washed hair sample was mixed with 10 ml 6.25% tetramethyl ammonium hydroxide (TMAH, Tama Chemical, Kawasaki, Japan) and 50 μl 0.1% gold solution (SPEX Certi Prep, Metuchen, NJ, USA), and then dissolved at 75 degrees C with shaking for 2 h. After cooling the solution to room temperature, internal standard (scandium, gallium, and indium) solution was added, and after adjusting its volume gravimetric, the obtained solution was used for multi-mineral analysis. The trace element concentrations were determined with inductively coupled plasma mass spectrometry (ICP-MS; 7500ce, Agilent Technologies, Santa Clara, CA, USA) as reported previously[6–8] and expressed as ng/g hair (ppb) or μg/g hair (ppm). Human hair-certified reference material (NIES CRM No. 13) was used to check for the accuracy of the analysis. The inter-daily variation of zinc, magnesium, calcium, aluminum, cadmium, lead, mercury, and arsenic determination was 2.2, 9.6, 6.3, 8.2, 6.9, 11.1, 9.4, and 6.9%, respectively. The control geometric mean value and reference range for each trace element were obtained from the data for 436 male healthy subjects aged 21-40 year old, as previously reported.[6,7,19,20]

The study was conducted in accordance with the Declaration of Helsinki and approved by the Institutional Ethics Committee of La Belle Vie Research Laboratory. All of the data obtained are held securely in such a form as to ensure anonymity.

Statistical analysis

Because each trace element concentration in scalp hair was almost log-normally distributed, the mineral concentration was converted to a logarithm, and the geometric rather than arithmetic mean is used as a representative of its hair concentration. The relation between high-burdened metal and zinc concentration or zinc/iron ratio of the subjects was examined by Pearson's correlation coefficient test.

Results

Zinc and magnesium deficiency in children with autistic disorders

Total 2550 children with autistic disorders (2108 males and 442 females aged 0-15 year old) were investigated. The histogram of hair logarithmic zinc concentrations for the autistic subjects was non-symmetric with tailing in the lower range, and 790 in 2550 subjects (31.0%) were found to have lower zinc concentration than -2 SD (standard deviation) level of the reference range [86.3-193 μg/g hair (ppm); geometric mean = 129 ppm], defined as zinc deficiency (Fig. 1). The incidence rate of zinc deficiency in the age group of 0-3-year-old was in the high range of 42-58%, with the mean rate of 43.9 and 55.8% in male and female, respectively (Fig. 2). In the 4-9 years old group, zinc deficiency rate is decreasing from over 40 to 10% or less. In the group aged 10-15 years old, zinc deficiency rate is remaining at a lower level, and the mean rate in male and female was 3.7 and 6.6%, respectively, indicating that infants are more susceptible to zinc deficiency than elder children. The minimum zinc concentration of 10.7 ppm detected in a 2-year-old boy corresponded to 1/12 of the mean reference level.

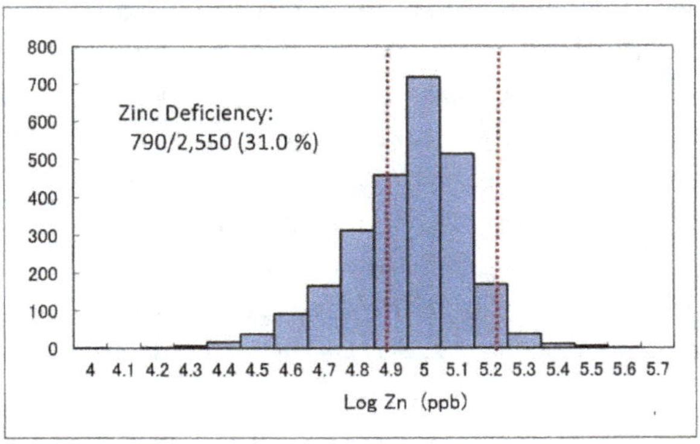

Fig. 1 Histogram of logarithmic zinc concentration in autistic children. The numbers on the abscissa indicate the logarithms of scalp hair zinc concentrations (ng/g: ppb). The height of each rectangle represents the frequency in the class interval in logarithmic hair zinc level. Two dotted vertical lines represent the -2 and +2 SD level of the reference range of hair zinc concentrations. The histogram of scalp hair zinc concentrations for 2550 children (2108 males and 442 females) aged 0-15

years is shown.

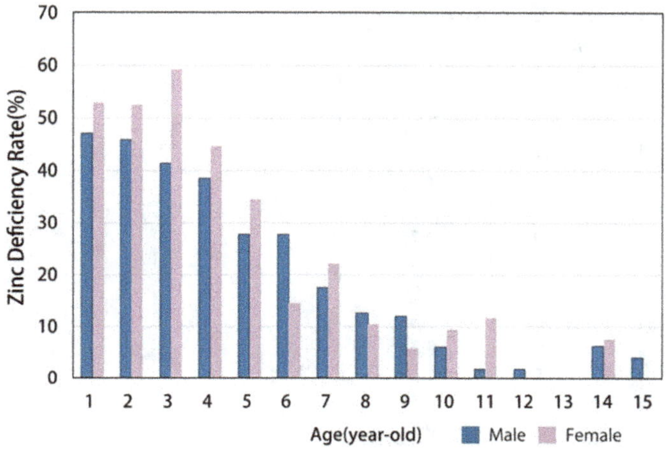

Fig. 2 Age-related prevalence rate of zinc deficiency in autistic children. The association of zinc deficiency rate with age (1-15 years old) in autistic subjects (*N* = 2550) is shown. The height of each rectangle represents the rate of zinc deficiency (%) in the respective age group.

Following to zinc deficiency, magnesium and calcium deficiency was observed in 477 (18.7%) and 137 (5.4%) individuals in the autistic children (Table 1), and for the other essential metals, such as iron, chromium, copper, manganese, and molybdenum, their incidence rates of deficiency were 1% or less. The incidence rate of magnesium deficiency in the age groups of 0-3, 4-9, and 10-15 years old is 26.3, 17.9, and 3.7% in male and 23.1, 16.4, and 1.3% in female subjects, respectively, suggesting that infants are also liable to magnesium deficiency than elder children. The minimal magnesium concentration of 3.88 ppm detected in a 2-year-old girl corresponds to almost 1/10 of the mean reference level (39.5 ppm). Calcium deficiency was observed in lower age groups <10-year-old.

Table 1. Incidence rate of mineral deficiency in autistic children		
	Cases with deficiency	
Mineral	Number	Rate (%)
Zn	790	30.98
Mg	477	18.71
Ca	137	5.37
Se	47	1.84
Co	42	1.65
Na	19	0.75
Fe	17	0.67
K	14	0.55
Cr	13	0.51
I	8	0.31
Cu	5	0.20
Mn	4	0.16
Mo	1	0.04

The number and incidence rate of individuals with mineral deficiency (lower than the -2 SD level of each reference range) in 2550 autistic children are tabled.

Toxic metal burdens in children with autistic disorders

In contrast, some toxic metals such as aluminum, cadmium, and lead highly accumulated over their +2 SD levels, in the individuals of 444 (17.4%), 221 (8.7%), and 114 (4.5%), and their incidence rates were higher than that of arsenic and mercury (2.5 and 1.6%, respectively) (Table 2). The detected maximal level of aluminum, cadmium, and lead was 79.4 ppm in a 4-year-old boy, 5.47 ppm in a 5-year-old boy and 24.9 ppm in a 5-year-old girl, respectively, corresponding to 21-, 782- and 57-fold of each mean reference level. The maximal burden level of mercury and arsenic of 40.1 ppm and 1.7 ppm, respectively, corresponds to 10- and 33-fold of the mean reference level.

Table 2. Incidence rate of high toxic metal burden in autistic children				
	Cases with high burden		Maximal concentration	
	Number	Rate (%)	(ppb)	Ratio to reference
Al	444	17.4	79400	21
Cd	221	8.7	5470	782
Pb	114	4.5	24900	57
As	65	2.5	1700	33
Hg	44	1.6	40100	10
Ni	29	1.1	4765	30

The number and incidence rate of individuals with high toxic metal burden (higher than +2 SD) in 2550 autistic children are tabled, with the maximum and ratio to reference level.

Essential metal burdens in children with autistic disorders

It is surprising that some essential heavy metals were highly burdened in the autistic children, as well as toxic metals. High molybdenum burdens over their +2 SD reference level were observed in 922 autistic individuals (36.2%), and the maximal concentration of 1341 ppb was detected in a 7-year-old boy, corresponding to 48-fold of the mean reference level (Table 3). Next to molybdenum, iron, vanadium, manganese, zinc, and copper exhibited high burden over their +2 SD reference levels in the autistic individuals of 318 (12.5%), 272 (10.7%), 190 (7.5%), 69 (2.7%), and 55 (2.2%), respectively. The maximum concentration of iron (39.9 ppm), vanadium (2.6 ppm), manganese (14 ppm), zinc (495 ppm), and copper (346 ppm), corresponding to 6.5-, 212-, 130-, 3.8-, and 18-fold of each mean reference level, respectively.

Table 3. Incidence of high burden of essential metals and the maximum level in autistic children

Mineral	High Burden Number	Rate (%)	Maximum (ppb)	Ratio to Ref.
Mo	922	36.2	1341	48
Fe	318	12.5	39850	7
V	272	10.7	603	212
Mn	190	7.5	14030	130
Zn	69	2.7	494600	4
K	64	2.5	1075000	65
Cu	55	2.2	345900	18
Cr	48	1.9	2105	39
I	34	1.3	253700	854
Na	30	1.2	597100	30
Co	27	1.1	3477	679
Ca	21	0.8	3745000	10
Mg	19	0.7	475700	12
Se	6	0.2	47300	70
Li	5	0.2	128	78

The number and incidence rate of individuals with high burden (over than +2 SD) in 2550 autistic children and the maximum concentration are tabled.

For the other burden metals, even though their prevalence was $<2.0\%$, the maximal levels detected were over 10-fold of the mean reference level, and some elements such as chromium, cobalt, and lithium reached to an extra-ordinal high level of 39-, 679-, and 78-fold of the mean reference level, respectively, suggesting the possibility of their adverse effects even though essential elements.

Relationships between zinc deficiency and high-burden metals

It is notable that there were significant relationships between zinc deficiency and some toxic metal burdens: the burden levels of lead, aluminum, cadmium, and arsenic inversely correlated to zinc concentration (r = -0.339, -0.247, -0.198, and -0.143, respectively; $P < 0.001$) (Fig. 3).

Furthermore, a more intimate inverse relationship was observed between zinc and molybdenum concentration (r = -0.509, $P < 0.00001$) (Fig. 4).

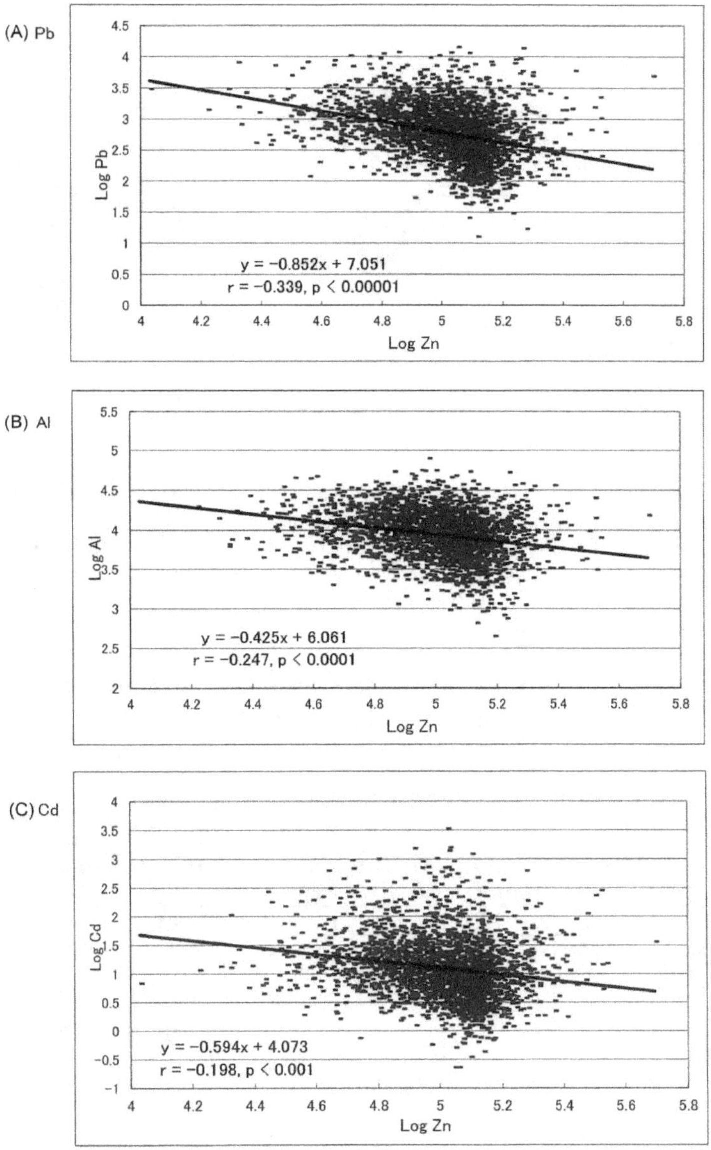

Fig. 3 Inverse relationship between zinc and toxic metal levels in autistic children. The inverse relationship between hair logarithmic zinc and (a) lead, (b) aluminum, and (c) cadmium concentrations in autistic children (N = 2550) is shown. Each point represents the corresponding logarithmic zinc and lead, aluminum, or cadmium concentration of the individual child. A highly significant inverse relationship between zinc and lead, aluminum, or cadmium concentrations (r = -0.339, -0.247 or -0.198, $P < 0.001$) in the autistic children is shown.

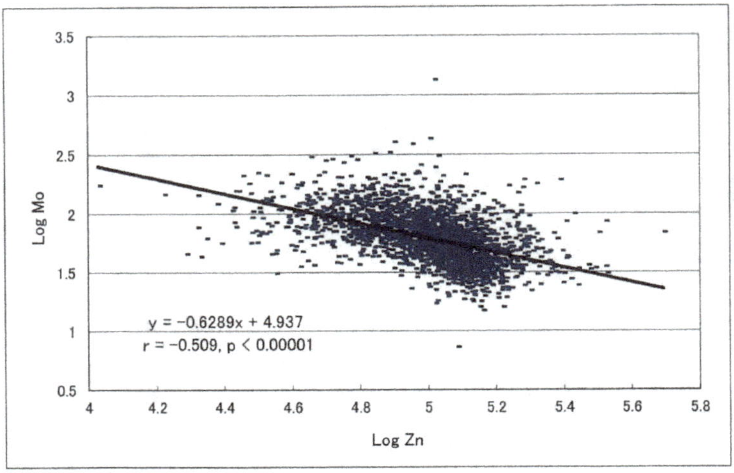

Fig. 4 Inverse relationship between zinc and molybdenum concentration in autistic children. The inverse relationship between hair logarithmic zinc and molybdenum concentration in autistic children (N = 2550) is shown. Each point represents the corresponding logarithmic zinc and molybdenum concentration of the individual child. A highly significant inverse relationship between zinc and molybdenum concentrations (r = -0.509, P < 0.00001) in the autistic children is shown.

As well as zinc, magnesium also exhibited a significant inverse correlation with some burdened metals such as not only arsenic, aluminum, and lead (r = -0.273, -0.159, and -0.142, respectively; P < 0.001) but also molybdenum (r = -0.387) (Table 4).

Table 4. Inverse relationships of toxic metals with zinc and magnesium in autistic children: Correlation matrix

	Zn	Pb	Al	Cd	Hg	As	Mg
Zn	1.000	−0.339	−0.247	−0.197	0.069	−0.143	0.526
Pb		1.000	0.451	0.609	−0.064	0.063	−0.142
Al			1.000	0.376	−0.082	−0.015	−0.159
Cd				1.000	−0.105	0.051	−0.048
Hg					1.000	0.104	0.064
As						1.000	−0.273

There was a mild inverse correlation of zinc with chromium and iron concentration (r = -0.205 and -0.154, respectively; P < 0.001) observed, but no inverse correlation either between zinc and copper (r = 0.081) or between molybdenum and copper (r = 0.058) was observed in the autistic subjects. It is emphasized that zinc is only one heavy essential metal exhibiting inverse correlations with various toxic and heavy metals, suggesting that this element can compete and antagonize toxic metals and plays the pivotal or gatekeeper role in bio-metal homeostasis.

One case in only two 0-year-old individuals (10-month-old female) in 2550 subjects was assessed as suffering from zinc and magnesium deficiency of 79.1 ppm (0.6-fold of the mean reference level) and 15.0 ppm (0.4-fold), with a high molybdenum burden of 220 ppb (7.8-fold), corresponding to nearly 2-fold of its +3 SD level (Fig. 5).

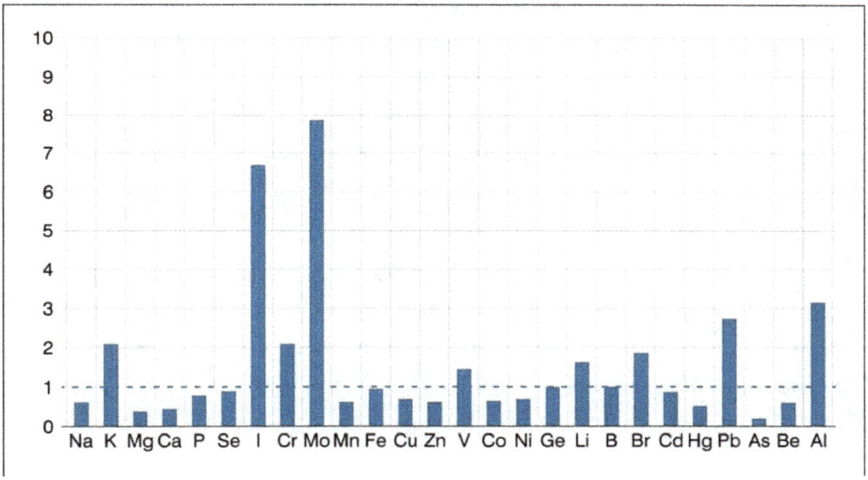

Fig. 5 Metallome profile of a 10-month-old girl with high molybdenum burden. Metallome profile of an autistic infant with zinc and magnesium deficiency and molybdenum burden. Each bar represents the relative concentration of the respective trace element in her scalp hair specimen. The dotted horizontal line at 1.0 represents the reference control level of each trace element.

Zinc/iron and zinc/copper ratio

As well as the zinc level itself, the ratio of zinc/iron (Zn/Fe ratio) seems to be a useful biomarker for assessing neurodevelopment disorders in Japanese autistic children examined: 671 individuals (26.3%) exhibited a lower ratio than its -2 SD level (Zn/Fe = 9.90), and the minimum ratio of 0.78 corresponded to 1/27 of the mean reference level of 21.0 (Fig. 6).

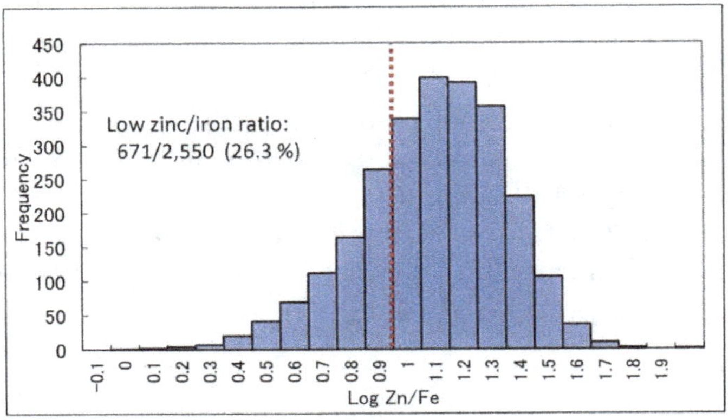

Fig. 6 Histograms of the zinc/iron ratio in autistic children. The histogram of the zinc/iron ratio for 2550 children is shown in the logarithm. The numbers on the abscissa indicate the logarithms of the zinc/iron ratio. The height of each rectangle represents the frequency in the class interval in the logarithmic zinc/iron ratio. The dotted vertical lines represent the -2 SD level of the reference range of hair zinc/iron ratio.

Furthermore, zinc/iron ratio exhibited a high-significant inverse-relationship with aluminum (r = -0.551), lead (r = -0.486), cadmium (r = -0.369, $P < 0.00001$), and molybdenum (r = -0.548) concentrations (Fig. 7).

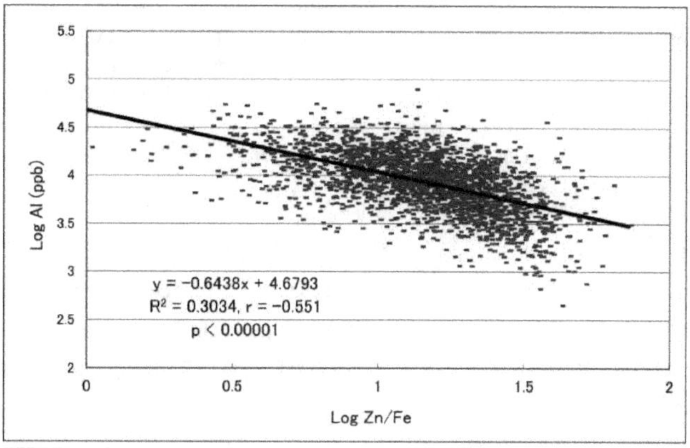

Log Al (ppb)
Log Zn/Fe
y = −0.6438x + 4.6793
R² = 0.3034, r = −0.551
p < 0.00001

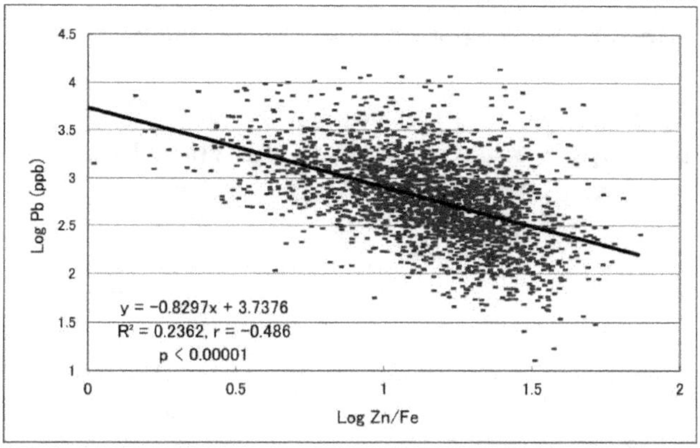

Log Pb (ppb)
Log Zn/Fe
y = −0.8297x + 3.7376
R² = 0.2362, r = −0.486
p < 0.00001

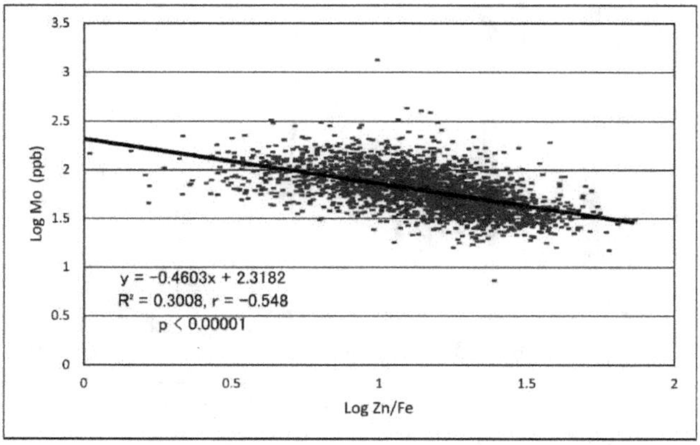

Log Mo (ppb)
Log Zn/Fe
y = −0.4603x + 2.3182
R² = 0.3008, r = −0.548
p < 0.00001

Fig. 7 Inverse relationship between zinc/iron ratio and toxic metal concentration. The inverse relationship between the logarithmic zinc/iron ratio and (a) aluminum, (b) lead, and (c) molybdenum concentrations in autistic children (N = 2550) is shown. Each point represents the corresponding logarithmic zinc/iron ratio and (a) aluminum, (b) lead, and (c) molybdenum concentration of the individual child. A highly significant inverse relationship between the zinc/iron ratio and aluminum, lead, cadmium, and molybdenum concentrations (r = -0.551, -0.486, and -0.548, respectively, $P < 0.00001$) in the autistic children is shown.

In contrast, on the zinc/copper ratio (Zn/Cu) reported as a good blood plasma biomarker for autism, there was less close correlation to the disorders in this study for Japanese subjects: the incidence rate of the individuals exhibiting lower ratios than 1.83 of its -2 SD level was as a few as 4.5% (115 in the 2550 autistic subjects), compared to the incidence of 26.3 and 31.0% based on the zinc/iron ratio and zinc concentration itself, respectively.

One rare case suffering from a high copper burden of 200 ppm, with a low zinc/copper ratio of 0.48, is shown in Fig. 8, in which co-burdens of chromium, molybdenum, lithium, etc. were detected.

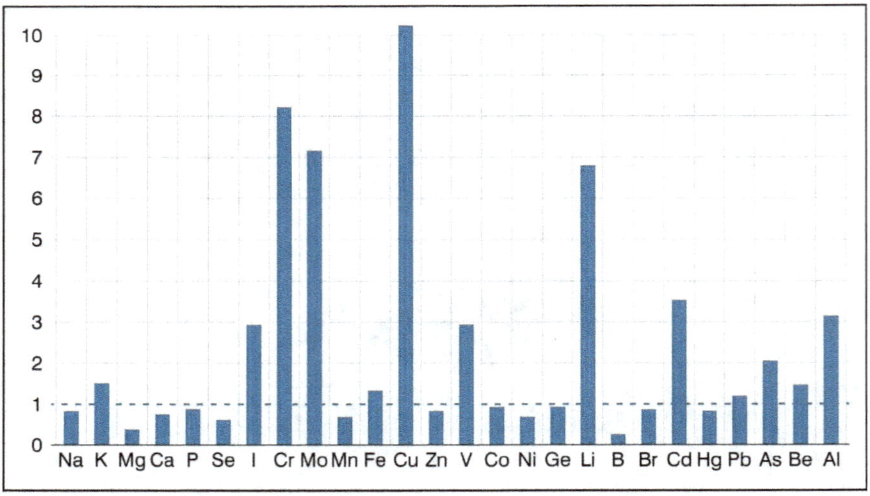

Fig. 8 Metallome profile of a 2-year-old boy with the high copper burden. Metallome profile of an autistic infant suffering from high burdens of copper, chromium,

molybdenum, lithium, and so on. Each bar represents the relative concentration of the respective trace element in his scalp hair specimen. The dotted horizontal line at 1.0 represents the reference control level of each trace element.

Discussion

Metallomics analysis for early assessment of neurodevelopmental disorders

Zinc is well accepted as an essential trace element, which functions as the active center in 300 kinds of enzymes and regulates the structure and function of ~10% in the total gene-coded proteins named 'zinc-finger proteins', contributing to the interaction of genetic and environmental factors and transcriptional regulation. Thus, zinc is necessary for normal neurogenesis and migration, myelination, synaptogenesis, and regulation of neurotransmitter release in the fetal cortex, hippocampus, cerebellum, and the autonomic nervous system.[21–23] Recently, zinc has been shown to regulate the function of the brain Shank family proteins, 'Shank2 and Shank3', and also prenatal zinc deficiency reduced the expression levels of these proteins, suggesting that these Shank proteins act as mediators of zinc effects on synaptic function.[10,11,14] Furthermore, it is hypothesized that zinc is well positioned to serve as a dynamic regulator to activate Shank-dependent pathways in synapse formation and plasticity in developing neurons[14] and that zinc deficiency is a key epigenetic factor in the etiology of ASD.[6–9,10–20]

In addition, dietary restriction-induced zinc deficiency has been reported to up-regulate intestinal zinc-importer (Zip4) and induce the increase in Zip4 protein located in the plasma membrane of enterocytes.[24,25] This adoptive response to zinc deficiency is known to lead to increasing in the risk of high-uptake of toxic metals such as cadmium and lead. Thus, infants with zinc deficiency are liable to be exposed to an increased risk of absorbing high amounts of toxic metals and retaining them in their body, as shown by the inverse relationships (Fig. 2). These findings suggest that the increased risk of toxic metal burdens attendant on the infantile zinc deficiency seem also synergistically contribute to the pathogenesis of neurodevelopmental disorders.[7–12]

Early diagnosing neurodevelopmental disorders such as ASD and ADHD was difficult since there was no clinical biochemical test, like a blood test, to diagnose the disorders. Therefore, autism was not usually diagnosed until after age 2, when delays in a child's social behavior and language skills become apparent, and many children cannot receive a final diagnosis and treatment until much older. This delay means that children with neurodevelopmental disorders fail to get the help needed and fail to have the chance of intervention/treatment in the narrow time window of mal-neurodevelopment and for therapy.

Thus, neuroscientists and psychologists use terms such as 'critical or sensitive period', 'infantile time window', or 'the first 1000 days' to describe time epoch of neurodevelopment/ vulnerability and opportunity for intervention/therapy.[6–9,26–28] This critical period is typically conceptualized as an early life epoch when alterations to brain structure/function by several environmental epigenetic factors (e.g. zinc and magnesium deficiency and various toxic metal or chemical substance burdens) result in irreversible long-term consequences.[6–9] The critical term 'sensitive period' or 'infantile time window' can also be used in a positive manner to describe the time window when the brain tissue is particularly receptive to positive nutritional or social intervention.[9,28] Both concepts rely on the observation that the younger, rapidly developing brain is more vulnerable than the elder brain, and also retains a greater degree of plasticity (e.g. recoverability). Although the distinction may become less meaningful, either concept emphasizes the need for pediatricians to focus on making sure the child is receiving adequate nutrition to promote normal brain development in a timely fashion.[6–9,12,28]

Thus, Insel proposed 'The sooner we are able to identify early markers for autism, the more effective our treatment/ interventions can be.[29] Policymakers also have recently placed a great deal of emphasis on the 'first 1000 days' and '0-3 years' as golden opportunities to influence child outcomes.

In an exploring study using validated tooth-matrix biomarkers, Arora *et al.* and Curtin *et al.* suggested that essential mineral deficiencies such as manganese and zinc and toxic metal burden of lead during specific developmental windows (both fetal and infantile) increase ASD risk and severity, supporting the hypothesis of systemic mineral imbalances in ASD and suggesting critical roles of fetal and postnatal metal dysregulation in the brain mal-development, and suggesting that altered zinc-copper rhythmicity precedes the emergence of ASD.[12,13]

As shown in Table 2, aluminum is the most high-burdened toxic metal in the autistic subjects examined. On this toxic metal, the group of Exley reported that the aluminum content of brain tissue in autism was consistently high, as well as in the patients with Alzheimer's disease and multiple sclerosis.[30–33] Furthermore, Lyons-Weiler and Ricketson reported that infants receive 17 times more aluminum than would be allowed if doses were adjusted per body weight, and several critical mistakes have been made in the consideration of pediatric dosing of aluminum contained in vaccines.[34]

It is notable that not only toxic but also some essential metals are highly burdened in the autistic children, as shown in Table 3. The high burdens of 'redox metals' such as iron, manganese, and copper, which have a characteristic of producing a reactive oxygen species 'hydroxyl radical' by the Fenton reaction, probably play critical roles in the pathogenesis of neurodevelopmental disorders, as well as in neurodegeneration diseases such as Parkinson's, Alzheimer diseases, multiple sclerosis, and amyotrophic lateral sclerosis.[35–42]

High molybdenum burden and its close inverse relationship with zinc in autistic children (Table 3 and Fig. 3) suggest that the overloading of molybdenum is probably another factor inducing zinc deficiency. And these findings accord with the fact that the patients with ASD and ADHD are comorbid with atopic dermatitis and food allergy, and they are inevitable to take soybean foods rich in molybdenum, as protein sources, in place of milk and eggs. In fact, in a large population-based survey of children's health in the USA and Taiwan, a striking association between atopic dermatitis and autism (OR: 3.04 and Hazard ratio: 16.6, respectively) is demonstrated.[43,44] These findings suggest that assessment of mineral imbalances (or dysregulation) in the child population is helpful for early diagnosis and open a novel therapeutic pathway for treating children suffering from not only neurodevelopmental disorders but also allergic diseases such as atopic dermatitis, food allergy, and asthma.

Faber *et al.* reported that the mean plasma Zn/Cu ratio in 230 children with autistic disorder is below the cut-off value of the lowest 2.5% of healthy children, and the zinc/copper ratio has been used as a helpful biomarker of heavy metal toxicity in children with ASD.[38,39–41] While, in our study for 2550 Japanese autistic children, the zinc/copper ratio was not closely correlated to autistic disorders: only just 4.5% (115 individuals) showed lower ratios than its cut-off (-2 SD) level, compared to the incidence rate of 31.0% based on the zinc deficiency itself. Instead of the zinc/copper ratio, the ratio of zinc/iron was found to be a good biomarker candidate for assessing autistic children: 26.3% (671 individuals) exhibited lower ratios than its -2 SD level (Fig. 5), and the minimum was 0.78 corresponding to as low as 1/27 of the mean reference ratio of 21.0. Furthermore, the zinc/iron ratio is more high-significantly inversely correlated with aluminum (r = -0.551), lead (r = -0.486), cadmium (r = -0.369), and molybdenum (r = -0.548, $P < 0.00001$) concentration (Fig. 6), suggesting that this Zn/Fe ratio is a useful biomarker as well as zinc itself for Japanese children with the neurodevelopmental disorders. These findings suit the reports on risk of iron-fortified infant formula and supplements in pregnancy and childhood.[45,46]

The gap of zinc/copper ratio data between in the Faber study and in our study is probably explained by the following two circumstances: that is, the first is the difference in the ingestion of inorganic copper from drinking water and taking a high-fat diet and cacao bean products such as cocoa and chocolates,[41] and the second is the difference in the zinc and copper contents in the follow-up milk products used in the USA and Japan, which are given to the infants over 6-month. In the milk products supplied in the USA and also Europe, zinc, and copper (5.5 and 0.4 mg/100 g powder milk) are co-supplemented with iron (7 mg/100 g), but in the Japanese products the mean iron content is as high as 9 mg/100 g (8.3-9.6 mg/100 g) and neither zinc nor copper is supplemented.[47,48] Therefore, it is supposed that the infants given Japanese follow-up milk products are suspected liable to zinc deficiency and iron excess, and the infants given US/European products are liable to copper excess or zinc/copper ratio decrease. Thus, many of the Japanese autistic children, especially infants, exhibit zinc deficiency and marginal iron excess with zinc/iron ratio decreasing, with less zinc/copper ratio decreasing, as shown in Fig. 6. In contrast, in US/European countries taking copper-rich foods and water and giving zinc and copper co-supplemented follow-up milk to babies, zinc/copper ratio decreasing has been reported useful and estimated as a good biomarker for autism.[38–41]

Early intervention/therapy: metallomics-based supplementation of nutrients

Zinc deficiency has been remarked in not only developing but also developed countries, through imbalanced intake of nutrients and dieting.[6,19,21,49] However, there are a few controlled clinical stud- ies on the supplementation of deficient minerals for the children with neurodevelopmental disorders. A valuable controlled clinical study on zinc supplementation for autistic elder children has been reported by Russo and Devito.[39] They report that high plasma cop- per levels in the patients with autism and pervasive developmental disorder (PDD) (mean age: 11.7 years) decreased to the normal level, and the severity of symptoms (e.g. awareness, receptive language, focus and attention, and hyperactivity, etc.) significantly decreased in autistic individuals following zinc and B-6 therapy. The beneficial effect of zinc on infantile neurodevelopment has been reported in a randomized, controlled trial of Peruvian infants aged 6-18 months, where zinc supplementation has been shown to sustain normative neurodevelopment.[50]

Arnold *et al.* report that the mean serum zinc level in children was significantly lower in ADHD group, and that serum zinc level correlated inversely with parent- and teacher-rated inattention in ADHD children.[51,52] Furthermore, zinc treatment was reported significantly superior to a placebo in reducing symptoms of hyperactivity, impulsivity, and impaired socialization in ADHD patients.[53,54] Another preliminary human study showed that many children with ADHD have lower zinc concentration in comparison to healthy children, and zinc supplement as an adjunct to methylphenidate has favorable effects in the treatment of ADHD children, pointing to the possible association between zinc deficiency and ADHD pathophysiology.[55]

Kozielec *et al.* have reported that in 116 hyperactive children with ADHD, magnesium deficiency was found in 95% of the subjects, most frequently in hair (77.6%), next in red blood cells (58.6%), and in blood serum (33.6%).[56] Furthermore, they reported that in the group of ADHD children given 6 months of magnesium supplementation, a significant decrease in hyperactivity and increase in hair magnesium contents has been achieved.[57] Mousain-Bosc *et al.* also reported that 52 hyper-excitable children have low intra-erythrocyte magnesium levels with normal serum magnesium values and that magnesium/vitamin B6 supplementation can restore the erythrocyte magnesium levels to normal and improve their abnormal behaviors.[58] They also reported that 33 children with clinical symptoms of PDD or autism exhibit significantly lower red blood cell magnesium values, and that the combination therapy with magnesium/vitamin B6 for 6 months significantly improved PDD symptoms in 23/33 children ($P < 0.0001$) with concomitant increases in intra-erythrocyte magnesium values.[59]

We also have experienced considerable cases of autistic children improved by the nutritional intervention supplementing deficient nutrients, on the basis of metallomics analysis (unpublished). The therapeutic efficacy of the evidence-based micronutrient supplementation for children with neurodevelopmental disorders remains to be demonstrated by a large double-blinded controlled study.

Conclusion and perspective

In this metallomics study for 2550 autistic children, we demonstrate that many of them are suffering from zinc and magnesium deficiency and marked high burdens of not only toxic but also some essential metals such as molybdenum, iron, manganese, and copper, especially in the early life of 0-3 years old, a critical period of a narrow 'infantile time window' in mal-neurodevelopment. Furthermore, it is notable that many of the highly burdened heavy metals detected in the autistic children have close relationships with the deficiency of the restricted essential elements (zinc and magnesium), and these findings suggest that supplementation of these deficient nutrients is helpful for intervention/therapy.

Thus, the early assessment of various profiles of body mineral imbalances, especially during the critical time window is useful for early diagnosis of neurodevelopmental disorders and probably for evidence-based individualized therapy of the patients during the therapeutic time window.

We hope that early assessment of mineral imbalances of individuals opens an avenue of evidence-based personalized precision medicine for neurodevelopmental disorders and also for the comorbid such as allergic immune diseases, in this decade.

Acknowledgements

The authors appreciate the subjects and their parents for their cooperation. They thank the laboratory team for their technical contributions to the trace element analysis.

References

1. V. Hughes, Autism: complex disorder, *Nature*, 2012, 491, S2–S3.
2. A. Krishnan, R. Zhang, V. Yao, C. L. Theesfeld, A. K. Wong, A. Tadych, N. Volfovsky, A. Packer, A. Lash and O. G. Troyanskaya,

Genome-wide prediction and functional characterization of the genetic basis of autism spectrum disorder, *Nat. Neurosci.*, 2016, 19, 1454–1462.

3. L. A. Sealey, B. W. Hughes, A. N. Sriskanda, J. R. Guest, A. D. Gibson, L. Johnson-Williams, D. G. Pace and O. Bagasra, Environmental factors in the development of autism spectrum disorders, *Environ. Int.*, 2016, 88, 288–298.

4. Centers for Disease Control and Prevention: Autism Spectrum Disorder (ASD): Data and Statistics. https://www.cdc.gov/mmwr/volumes/70/ss/ss7011a1.htm (3 December 2021, date last accessed)

5. J. P. Goulle, L. Mahieu, J. Castermant, N. Neveu, L. Bonneau, G. Laine, D. Bouige and C. Lacroix, Metal and metalloid multi-elementary ICP-MS validation in whole blood, plasma, urine and hair: reference values, *Forens. Sci. Intern.*, 2005, 153, 39–44.

6. H. Yasuda, K. Yoshida, Y. Yasuda and T. Tsutsui, Infantile zinc deficiency: association with autism spectrum disorders, *Sci. Rep.*, 2011, 1, 129.

7. H. Yasuda, Y. Yasuda and T. Tsutsui, Estimation of autistic children by metallomics analysis, *Sci. Rep.*, 2013, 3, 1199.

8. H. Yasuda and T. Tsutsui, Assessment of infantile mineral imbalances in autism spectrum disorders (ASDs), *Int. J. Environ. Res. Public Health*, 2013, 10, 6027–6043.

9. H. Yasuda, Early assessment and intervention of mineral imbalances for autistic children, In: A Valdez (ed), *Autism Spectrum Disorders*, Nova Sci Pub, 2015, pp. 27–49.

10. S. Grabrucker, L. Jannetti, M. Eckert, S. Gaub, R. Chhabra, S. faender, K. Mangus, P. P. Reddy, V. Rankovic, M. J. Schmeisser, M. R. Kreutz, G. Ehret, T. M. Boeckers and A. M. Grabrucker, Zinc deficiency dysregulates the synaptic ProSAP/Shank scaffold and might contribute to autism spectrum disorders. *Brain*, 2014, 137, 137–152.

11. A. M. Grabrucker, A role of synaptic zinc in ProSAP/Shank PSD scaffold malformation in autism spectrum disorders, *Dev. Neurobiol.*, 2014, 74, 136–146.

12. M. Arora, A. Reichenberg, C. Willfors, C. Austin, C. Gennings, S. Berggren, P. Lichtenstein, H. Anckarsäter, K. Tammimies and S. Bölte,

Fetal and postnatal metal dysregulation in autism, *Nat. Commun.*, 2017, 8, 15493.

13. P. Curtin, C. Austin, A. Curtin, C. Gennings, M. Arora, K. Tammimies, C. Willfors, S. Berggren, P. Siper, D. Rai, K. Meyering, A. Kolevzon, J. Mollon, A. S. David, G. Lewis, S. Zammit, L. Heilbrun, R. F. Palmer, R. O. Wright, S. Bölte and A. Reichenberg, Dynamical features in fetal and postnatal zinc-copper metabolic cycles predict the emergence of autism spectrum disorder, *Sci. Adv.*, 2018, 4, eaat1293.

14. H. T. T. Ha, S. Leal-Ortiz, K. Lalwani, S. Kiyonaka, I. Hamachi, S. P. Mysore, J. M. Montgomery, C. C. Garner, J. R. Huguenard and S. A. Kim, Shank and zinc mediate an AMPA receptor sub- unit switch in developing neurons, *Front. Mol. Neurosci.*, 2018, 11, 405.

15. E. Masini, E. Loi, A. F. Vega-Benedetti, M. Carta, G. Doneddu, R. Fadda and P. Zavattari, An overview of the main genetic, epigenetic and environmental factors involved in autism spectrum disorder focusing on synaptic activity, *Int. J. Mol. Sci.*, 2020, 21, 8290.

16. M. Fiore, R. Barone, C. Copat, A. Grasso, A. Cristaldi, R. Rizzo and M. Ferrante, Metal and essential element levels in hair and association with autism severity, *J. Trace Elem. Med. Biol.*, 2020, 57, 126409.

17. S. Hagmeyer, A. K. Sauer and A. M. Grabrucker, Prospects of zinc supplementation in autism spectrum disorders and Shankopathies such as Phelan McDermid syndrome, *Front. Synaptic. Neurosci.*, 2018, 10, 11.

18. H. Yasuda and T. Tsutsui, Assessment of infantile mineral imbalances in autism spectrum disorders (ASDs), In: C Croft (ed), *Environment Hazards and Neurodevelopment*, Apple Acad Press, 2015, pp. 153–173.

19. H. Yasuda and T. Tsutsui Infants and elderlies are susceptible to zinc deficiency. *Sci. Rep.*, 2016, 6, 21850.

20. H. Yasuda, T. Tsutsui and K. Suzuki, Metallomics analysis for assessment of toxic metal burdens in infants/children and their mothers: early assessment and intervention are essential, *Biomolecules*, 2021, 11, 6.

21. A. S. Prasad, Impact of the discovery of human zinc deficiency on health, *J. Am. Coll. Nutr.*, 2009, 28, 257–265.

22. A. Takeda, Movement of zinc and its functional significance in the brain, *Brain Res. Rev.*, 2000, 34, 137–148.
23. I. Wessels, M. Maywald and L. Rink, Zinc as gatekeeper of immune function, *Nutrients*, 2017, 9, 1286.
24. J. Dufner-Beattie, Y.-M. Kuo, J. Gitschier and G. K. Andrews, The adaptive response to dietary zinc in mice involves the differential cellular localization and zinc regulation of the zinc transporters ZIP4 and ZIP5, *J. Biol. Chem.*, 2004, 279, 49082–49090.
25. L. A. Lichten and R. J. Cousins, Mammalian zinc transporters: nutritional and physiologic regulation, *Ann. Rev. Nutr.*, 2009, 29, 153–176.
26. M. H. Bornstein, Sensitive periods in development: structural characteristics and causal interpretations, *Psychol. Bull.*, 1989, 105, 179–197.
27. J. F. Werker and T. K. Hensch, Critical periods in speech perception: new directions, *Ann. Rev. Psychol.*, 2015, 66, 173–196.
28. S E. Cusick and M. K. Georgieff, The role of nutrition in brain development: the golden opportunity of the "First 1000 days", *J. Pediatr.*, 2016, 175, 16–21.
29. T. R. Insel, Mental disorders in childhood: shifting the focus from behavioral symptoms to neurodevelopmental trajectories, *JAMA*, 2014, 311, 1727–1728.
30. M. Mold, D. Umar, A. King and C. Exley, Aluminium in brain tissue in autism, *J. Trace Elem. Med. Biol.*, 2018, 46, 76–82.
31. A. Mirza, A. King, C. Troakes and C. Exley, Aluminium in brain tissue in familial Alzheimer's disease, *J. Trace Elem. Med. Biol.*, 2017, 40, 30–36.
32. M. Mold, A. Chmielecka, M. Rodriguez, F. Thom, C. Linhart, A. King and C. Exley, Aluminium in brain tissue in multiple sclero- sis, *Int. J. Environ. Res. Public Health*, 2018, 15, E1777.
33. G. Morris, B. K. Puri and R. E. Frye, The putative role of environmental aluminium in the development of chronic neuropathology in adults and children. How strong is the evidence and what could be the mechanisms involved? *Metab. Brain Dis.*, 2017, 32, 1335–1355.
34. J. Lyons-Weiler and R. Ricketson, Reconsideration of the immunotherapeutic pediatric safe dose levels of aluminum, *J. Trace*

Elem. Med. Biol., 2018, 48, 67–73.

35. X. Jiang, B. R. Stockwell and M. Conrad, Ferroptosis: mechanisms, biology and role in disease, *Nat. Rev. Molec. Cell Biol.*, 2021, 22, 266–282.

36. S. Sheykhansari, K. Kozielski, J. Bill, M. Sitti, D. Gemmati, P. Zamboni and A. V. Singh, Redox metals homeostasis in multiple sclerosis and amyotrophic lateral sclerosis: a review, *Cell Death Disease*, 2018, 9, 348.

37. G. J. Brewer, Alzheimer's disease causation by copper toxicity and treatment with zinc, *Front. Aging Neurosci.*, 2014, 6, 92.

38. S. Faber, G. M. Zinn, J. C. Kern Ii and H. M. Skip Kingston, The plasma zinc/serum copper ratio as a biomarker in children with autism spectrum disorders, *Biomarkers*, 2009, 14, 171–180.

39. A. J. Russo and R. Devito, Analysis of copper and zinc plasma concentration and the efficacy of zinc therapy in individuals with Asperger's syndrome, pervasive developmental disorder not otherwise specified (PDD-NOS) and autism, *Biomark Insights*, 2011, 6, 127–133.

40. S. O. Li, J. L. Wang, G. Bjørklund, W. N. Zhao and C. H. Yin, Serum copper and zinc levels in individuals with autism spectrum disorders, *Neuroreport*, 2014, 25, 1216–1220.

41. E. C. Craciun, G. Bjørklund, A. A. Tinkov, M. A. Urbina, A. V. Skalny, F. Rad and E. Dronca, Evaluation of whole blood zinc and copper levels in children with autism spectrum disorder, *Metab. Brain Dis.*, 2016, 31, 887–890.

42. Y. Nakagawa and K. Chiba, Involvement of neuroinflammation during drain development in social cognitive deficits in Au-tism spectrum disorder and schizophrenia, *J. Pharmacol. Exp. Ther.*, 2016, 358, 504–515.

43. P. Yaghmaie, C. W. Koudelka and E. L. Simpson, Mental health comorbidity in atopic dermatitis, *J. Allergy Clin. Immunol.*, 2013, 131, 428–433.

44. C. Y. Lee, M. H. Chen, M. J. Jeng, J. W. Hsu, S. J. Tsai, Y. M. Bai, G. Y. Hung, H. J. Yen, T. J. Chen and T. P. Su, Longitudinal association between early atopic dermatitis and subsequent attention-deficit or autistic disorder: a population-based case-control study, *Medicine (Baltimore)*, 2016, 95, e5005

45. B. Lozoff, Follow-up of a randomized controlled trial of iron-fortified (12.7 mg/L) vs low-iron (2.3 mg/L) infant formula: developmental outcome at 10 years, *Arch. Pediatr. Adolesc. Med.*, 2012, 166, 208–215.

46. M. K. Georgieff, N. F. Krebs and S. E. Cusick, The benefits and risks of iron supplementation in pregnancy and childhood, *Ann. Rev. Nutr.*, 2019, 39, 121–146.

47. H. Kodama, Trace element deficiency in infants and children: Clinical Practice, *Jpn. Med. Assoc. J.*, 2004, 47, 376–381.

48. N. F. Krebs, J. E. Westcott, D. L. Culbertson, L. Sian, L. V. Miller and K. M. Hambidge, Comparison of complementary feeding strategies to meet zinc requirements of older breastfed infants, *Am. J. Clin. Nutr.*, 2012, 96, 30–35.

49. R. S. Gibson, A.-L. M. Heath and E. A. Szymlek-Gay, Is iron and zinc nutrition a concern for vegetarian infants and young children in industrialized countries? *Am. J. Clin. Nutr.*, 2014, 100 (Suppl 1), 459S–468S.

50. J. Colombo, N. Zavaleta, K. N. Kannass, F. Lazarte, C. Albornoz, L. L. Kapa and L. E. Caulfield, Zinc supplementation sustained normative neurodevelopment in a randomized, controlled trial of Peruvian infants aged 6–18 months, *J. Nutr.*, 2014, 144, 1298–1305.

51. L. E Arnold, H. Bozzolo, J. Hollway, A. Cook, R. A. Disilvestro, D. R. Bozzolo, L. Crowl, Y. Ramadan and C. Williams, Serum zinc correlates with parent- and teacher-rated inattention in children with attention-deficit/hyperactivity disorder, *J. Child Adoles. Psychopharmacol.*, 2005, 15, 628–636.

52. L. E Arnold and R. A. Disilvestro, Zinc in attention-deficit/hyperactivity disorder, *J. Child Adolesc. Psychopharmacol.*, 2005, 15, 619–627.

53. O. Yorbik, M. F Ozdag, A. Olgun, M. G Senol, S. Bek and S. Akman, Potential effects of zinc on information processing in boys with attention deficit hyperactivity disorder, *Prog. Neuropsychopharm. Biol. Psychiatry*, 2008, 32, 662–667.

54. A. M. DiGirolamo, M. Ramirez-Zea, M. Wang, R. Flores-Ayala, R. Martorell, L. M. Neufeld, U. Ramakrishnan, D. Sellen, M. M. Black and A. D. Stein, Randomized trial of the effect of zinc supplementation

on the mental health of school-age children in Guatemala, *Am. J. Clin. Nutr.*, 2010, 92, 1241–1250.

55. S. Akhondzadeh, M.-R. Mohammadi and M. Khademi, Zinc sulfate as an adjunct to methylphenidate for the treatment of attention deficit hyperactivity disorder in children: a double blind and randomized trial [ISRCTN64132371], *BMC Psychiatry*, 2004, 4, 9–14.

56. T. Kozielec and B. Starobrat-Hermelin, Assessment of magnesium levels in children with attention deficit hyperactivity disorder (ADHD), *Magnes. Res.*, 1997, 10, 143–148.

57. B. Starobrat-Hermelin and T. Kozielec, The effects of magnesium physiological supplementation on hyperactivity in children with attention deficit hyperactivity disorder (ADHD). Positive response to magnesium oral loading test, *Magnes. Res.*, 1997, 10, 149–156.

58. M. Mousain-Bose, M. Roche, J. Rapin and J. P. Bali, Magnesium VitB6 intake reduces central nervous system hyperexcitability in children, *J Amer. Coll. Nutr.*, 2004, 23, S545–S548.

59. M. Mousain-Bose, M. Roche, A. Polge, D. Pradal-Prat, J. Rapin and J. P. Bali, Improvement of neurobehavioral disorders in children supplemented with magnesium-vitamin B6 II. Pervasive developmental disorder autism, *Magnes. Res.*, 2006, 19, 53–62.

Chapter 6:

TWO AGE-RELATED ACCUMULATION PROFILES OF TOXIC METALS

published in **Current Aging Science 5: 105-111 (2012).**

Hiroshi Yasuda, Kazuya Yoshida, Yuichi Yasuda and Toyoharu Tsutsui

Abstract: In order to investigate the body burden levels of toxic metals in Japanese, five toxic metal concentrations in scalp hair samples from 28,424 subjects from infant to elderly were determined with inductively coupled plasma mass spectrometry (ICP-MS). The geometric mean of hair mercury concentrations showed a high-significant age-correlated increase ($r = 0.341$, $p < 0.0001$) with a peak at the 6th decade of life and then decreased with further aging in both sexes. The mean mercury concentrations in male adults were significantly higher than those in female ($p < 0.001$), indicating the gender difference (male > female) in mercury accumulation. Arsenic also showed a similar accumulation profile with age-dependency and gender difference in adult subjects. In contrast, cadmium, lead and aluminium exhibited another type of accumulation profile: the highest burden level was observed in infants aged 0-3 years old for every element in both sexes. In addition, cadmium was found to have a character accumulating in aged females, with significant age-dependency ($r = 0.134$, $p < 0.0001$) and gender difference (female > male).

These findings suggest that toxic metals are classified into two families on the basis of their accumulation profiles, and that the three elements of mercury, arsenic and cadmium which accumulate age-dependently in adults, may play a role in aging process and higher burden with them may lead to acceleration of aging.

Keywords: Toxic metal accumulation, correlation with age, gender difference, mercury, arsenic, cadmium.

Introduction

Environmental pollution with toxic metals is one of the problems today. Hair is a unique tissue containing a special protein "hair-specific keratin" which is rich in cysteine capable of binding with toxic metals, and has a role of excreting them from the body. In fact, high toxic metal levels have been reported in the scalp hair samples from the subjects exposed to toxic metal pollutions, such as mercury, cadmium, arsenic or lead [1-4]. Thus, scalp hair is generally accepted as a biomarker specimen for estimating methyl- mercury exposure, and hair mineral analysis has been used in forensic medicine, in screening populations for toxic metal poisoning and in monitoring environmental pollutants [5-8]. In particular, Goulle *et al.* [7] have demonstrated that hair mineral analysis using a high specific and sensitive inductively coupled plasma mass spectrometry (ICP-MS) method is reliable and suitable for estimating chronic toxic metal pollution and mineral deficiency in human body. Thus, its clinical application has been tried for diagnosis of some diseases and symptoms [9-12].

The purpose of this study was to examine the burden levels of toxic metals in Japanese population. The data of representative five toxic metals including metalloid (mercury, arsenic, cadmium, lead and aluminium) in scalp hair samples from total 28,424 Japanese subjects aged 0-100 years were used, and their body burden levels were estimated. This study demonstrates that there are two age-related accumulation profiles for toxic metals and that the three elements of mercury, arsenic and cadmium accumulate with age-dependency and their accumulation may play a role in aging process.

Methods

Scalp Hair Samples and Toxic Metal Analysis

On the basis of informed consent, scalp hair samples from 28,424 (male: 9,612; female: 18,812) subjects aged 0-100 years were collected in the period from June 2005 to July 2007 (Table **1**). Hair sampling was recommended to cut as close to the scalp of the occipital area as possible. Hair sample of 75 mg was weighed into 50ml plastic tube, and washed with acetone and then with 0.01% Triton solution, in accordance with the procedures recommended by the Hair Analysis Standardization Board [13]. The washed hair sample was mixed with 10 ml 6.25% tetra methyl ammonium hydroxide (TMAH, Tama Chemical, Kawasaki, Japan) and 50 μl 0.1% gold solution (SPEX Certi Prep,

Metuchen, NJ, USA), and then dissolved at 75 C with shaking for 2 hours. After cooling of the solution to room temperature, internal standard (Sc, Ga, and In) solution was added, and after adjusting its volume gravimetrically to 15.0 g, the obtained solution was used for mineral analysis. The toxic metal and metalloid concentrations were determined with inductively coupled plasma mass spectrometry (ICP-MS; collision-typed 7500c, Agilent Technologies, Santa Clara, CA, USA) by the internal standard method as previously reported [10-12,14] and are expressed as ng/g hair (ppb). The detection limit was 16, 3.6, 2.2, 3.4 and 47 ppb for mercury, arsenic, cadmium, lead and aluminium, respectively. The inter-daily variation of analysis for mercury, arsenic, cadmium, lead and aluminium was calculated 9.4, 6.9, 15.2, 5.8 and 6.9 %, respectively.

Table 1. Tested Subjects (N = 28,424)

Age (year-old)	Female	Male
0-3	200	660
4-9	306	1,000
10-15	181	338
16-19	134	105
20-29	2,817	927
30-39	6,421	2,147
40-49	3,763	1,829
50-59	2,648	1,371
60-69	1,476	796
70-79	695	364
80-	171	75
Total	**18,812**	**9,612**

This study has been approved by review of the ethical committee of La Belle Vie Inc. All of the data obtained are held securely in such a form as to ensure anonymity.

Statistical Analysis

Because scalp hair toxic metal concentrations are lognormal distributed, geometric rather than arithmetic means were used as representative of their hair concentrations. The relation between the toxic metal concentrations and age of the subjects was investigated by Pearson's correlation coefficient test.

The statistically significant difference was determined using Welch's t-test.

Results

Five toxic metal concentrations in the scalp hair specimens from 28,424 subjects were distributed in nearly lognormal profile. Figure **1** for mercury exhibits a marked age-related accumulation profile with gender-difference (male > female) in adult subjects. The geometric mean of hair mercury concentrations in male adults showed a high-significant age-correlated increase ($r = 0.341$, $p < 0.0001$) from the lowest of around 2,000 ng/g (ppb) up to a peak of 5,700 ng/g at the 6th decade of life, and then decreased with further aging ($r = -0.170$, $p < 0.0001$) (Fig. **1**). Similar age-dependent profile

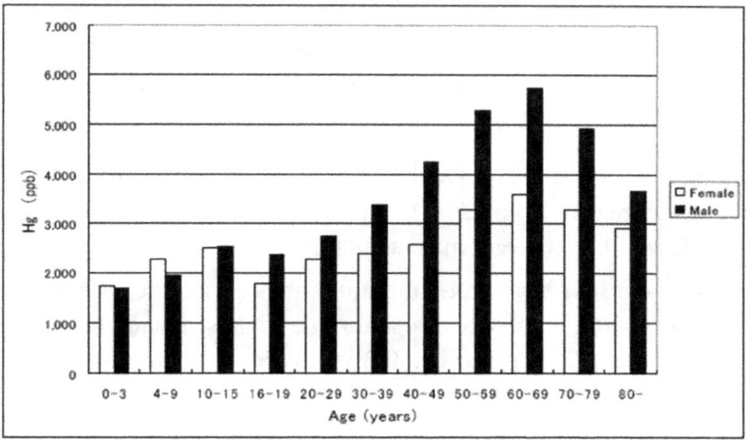

Fig. (1). Mean hair mercury concentrations in Japanese subjects (N = 28,424).
Each column represents the geometric mean of hair mercury concentrations (ng/g hair) for female and male subjects aged 0-3, 4-9, 10-15, 16-19, 20-29, 30-39, 40-49, 50-59, 60-69, 70-79 and 80 years over.

A similar, age-correlated accumulation profile with gender difference was observed for arsenic (Fig. **2**). In male adults, the mean arsenic concentrations increased age-dependently from around 50 ng/g to over 90 ng/g at 70's ($r = 0.109$, $p < 0.0001$), while in female, the mean levels increased from around 20 ng/g to over 40 ng/g.

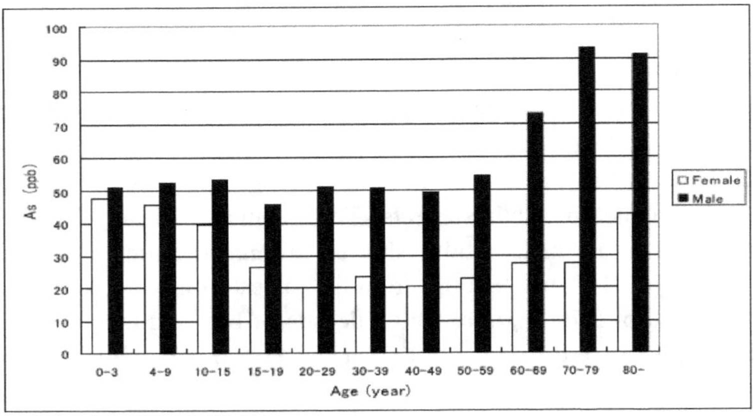

Fig. (2). Mean hair arsenic concentrations in Japanese subjects (N = 28,424).

Each column represents the geometric mean of hair arsenic concentrations (ng/g hair) for female and male subjects aged 0-3, 4-9, 10-15, 16-19, 20-29, 30-39, 40-49, 50-59, 60-69, 70-79 and 80 years over.

was also observed in female ($r = 0.217$, $p < 0.0001$): the mean mercury concentrations increased from 1,700 to 3,600 ng/g, although their levels were significantly lower than those in male adults ($p < 0.001$)

In contrast, cadmium, lead and aluminium showed another accumulation profile different from mercury and arsenic: the highest mean concentration was observed in the infant group aged 0-3 years for every element (Fig. **3-5**).

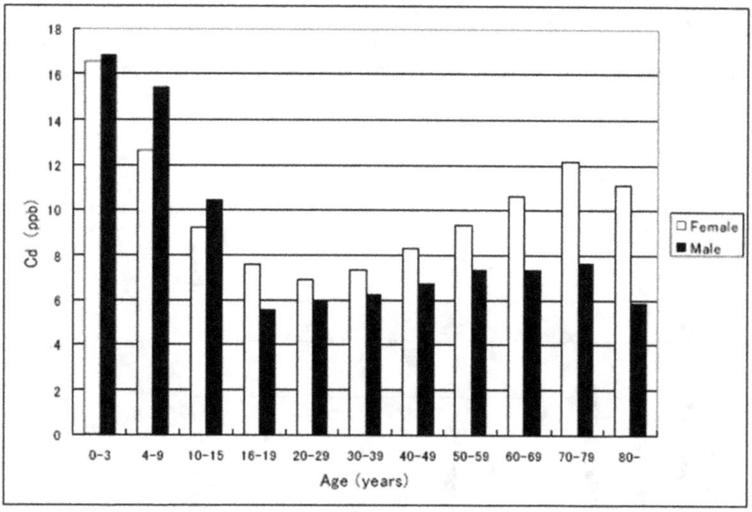

Fig. (3). Mean hair cadmium concentrations in Japanese subjects (N = 28,424).
Each column represents the geometric mean of hair cadmium concentrations (ng/g hair) for female and male subjects aged 0-3, 4-9, 10-15, 16-19, 20-29, 30-39, 40-49, 50-59, 60-69, 70-79 and 80 years over.

In addition, for cadmium a significant age-correlated accumulation ($r = 0.134$, $p < 0.0001$) was observed in female adults with a peak at the 7th decade of life and its mean burden levels in aged women were significantly ($p < 0.0001$) higher than those in male subjects (Fig. **3**).

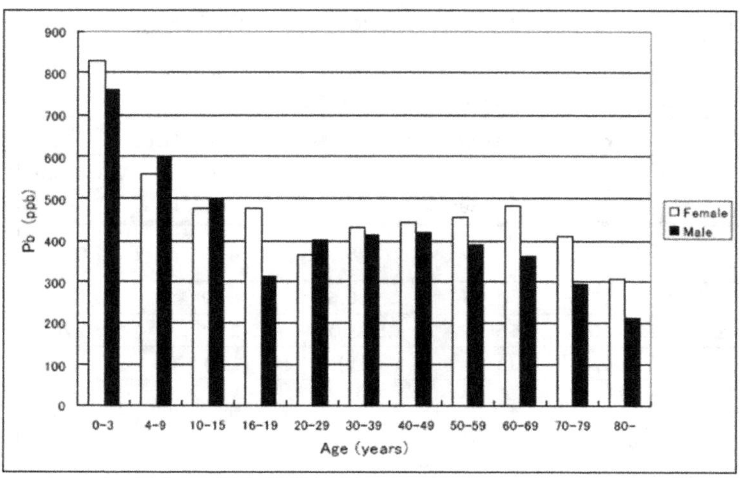

Fig. (4). Mean hair lead concentrations in Japanese subjects (N = 28,424).
Each column represents the geometric mean of hair lead concentrations (ng/g hair) for female and male subjects aged 0-3, 4-9, 10-15, 16-19, 20-29, 30-39, 40-49, 50-59, 60-69, 70-79 and 80 years over.

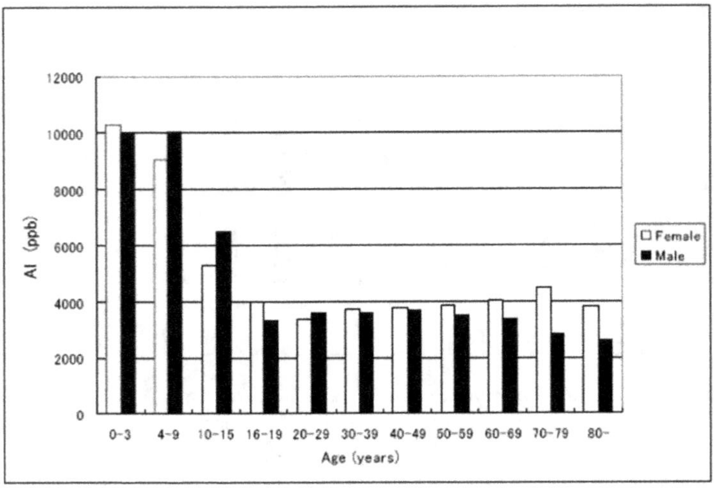

Fig. (5). Mean hair aluminium concentrations in Japanese subjects (N = 28,424).
Each column represents the geometric mean of hair aluminium concentrations (ng/g hair) for female and male subjects aged 0-3, 4-9, 10-15, 16-19, 20-29, 30-39, 40-49, 50-59, 60-69, 70-79 and 80 years over.

The maximum accumulation level of toxic metals in children was observed in the individuals aged 0-3 years for every toxic element (Table **2**).

Table 2. Maximum Accumulation Levels of Toxic Metals in Infants

Table 2. Maximum Accumulation Levels of Toxic Metals in Infants					
	Mercury	Arsenic	Cadmium	Lead	Aluminum
			Female		
Geomean in Adults	2,685	30.0	8.9	461	4,044
in Infants	1,725	47.6	16.6	829	10,318
Maximum Level	19,210	566.4	1,541.0	12,130	62,770
(Age)	(3-y)	(1-y)	(2-y)	(1-y)	(1-y)
			Male		
Geomean in Adults	3,894	51.0	7.0	434	3,758

in Infants	1,685	51.1	16.8	758	10,009
Maximum Level	36,280	394.1	1,972.0	29,480	74,310
(Age)	(2-y)	(1-y)	(2-y)	(2-y)	(2-y)
					ng/g (ppb)

In particular, the highest level of 1,972 ng/g for cadmium, which was detected in a 2-year-old boy, was estimated about 280-fold higher than the reference mean level in adults. For lead and aluminium, almost 68-fold and 20-fold higher level was detected in a different 2-year-old boy, respectively. Whereas, for mercury and arsenic, the highest level in children corresponded to only about 9- and 8-fold of the adult mean level, respectively.

Discussion

In the present toxic metallomic study, we estimated the body burden levels of five toxic metals including metalloid, namely neurotoxic mercury, lead and aluminium, and carcinogenic cadmium and arsenic, for 28,424 Japanese subjects from infant to elderly.

On the basis of the accumulation profile in the scalp hair specimens, toxic metals were grouped into two families. The first family composing of mercury and arsenic showed a characteristic profile of a marked age-dependency and gender difference (male > female) in adult subjects (Fig. 1 and 2). The second family including cadmium, lead and aluminium showed another characteristic profile exhibiting the highest accumulation in infants aged 0-3 years for both sexes (Fig. **3-5**), although only for cadmium a considerable age-correlated accumulation profile with inverse gender- difference (female > male) was observed.

On the mechanism of the gender difference for mercury and arsenic (male > female), it is reported that some sex hormonal control may be involved in human mercury uptake and elimination, because a marked sex difference in the tissue uptake and elimination was observed in methyl-mercury treated animals [15]. In addition, the lower level in female may be due to the low amounts of dietary fish consumption and high incidence of artificial hair waving among women [6,14,16].

The mechanism of the inverse gender difference for cadmium (female > male) may relate to its ability to form a high-affinity complex with estrogen receptor and exhibit potent estrogen-like activities [17]. Furthermore, the highest cadmium accumulation in the aged-female group at the 7th decade of life (Fig. **3**) explains the reason why many patients suffered from Itai-itai disease were senile women [18,19].

This study demonstrated that mercury exhibits the highest significant correlation to aging, with the regression coefficient of $r = 0.341$ in male and $r = 0.217$ in female ($p < 0.0001$). This finding suggests that mercury accumulation plays a considerable role in physiological senescence, particularly in Japanese, because mercury is well known to not only inhibit various enzyme reactions and metabolic processes but also enhance lipid peroxidation, progression of atherosclerosis and the risk of myocardial infarction and/or stroke [20-22]. We also reported that hair mercury concentration in male Japanese is significantly correlated to their body mass index [11], which is well accepted to be a risk factor associated with overall mortality. Probably, this correlation of mercury burden with body mass index may explain the reason why the peak of mercury accumulation appears at the 6th decade of life (Fig. 1), corresponding to that little senile persons with obesity are alive.

Table 2 demonstrates the probability of toxic metal pollution in infants: all of the highest accumulation levels detected in children were observed in infant individuals aged 0-3 years. In particular, the maximum burden level for cadmium (1,972 ng/g) in a 2-year-old boy corresponded to about 280-fold higher than the adult reference level. For lead and aluminium, the highest level of 29,480 ng/g and 74,310 ng/g corresponded to almost 68-fold and 20-fold of each reference level, respectively. Even for mercury and arsenic, a high level of 36,280 ng/g and 394 ng/g detected in the infant aged 1- and 2-year-old, respectively, corresponded to about 9-fold and 8-fold of the adult reference level. We have to consider that the mercury burden level of 36,280 ng/g is highly over the threshold of 14,000 ng/g (14 ppm) that is the upper limit recommended by FAO/WHO Meeting (JECFA2003).

The high accumulation of toxic metals in infants may be explained by their higher intestinal absorption and less effective renal excretion in newborns [23]. Freundlich *et al.* [24] reported that in two infants with severe kidney failure, the absorption and retention of aluminium from a cow's milk-based formula resulted in clinical toxicity. Thus, newborns and infants are likely at increased risk of absorbing high amount of toxic metals and retaining them in their bodies.

Another origin of these toxic metal accumulations in infants is presumed to be due to the cigarette smoking by their parents, in particular by the mothers [25-27]. Maternal cigarette smoking is reported to be associated with higher cadmium and lead and lower zinc concentrations in their neo- nates [28]. During pregnancy and lactation, these toxic metals accumulated in maternal bone tissues seem to be co-transferred with calcium to fetal and newborn bodies through increased bone-resorption [29,30].

In the present study on 5 toxic metal burdens, the three elements of mercury, arsenic and cadmium were found to show age-dependent accumulation profile, suggesting that these toxic elements may play a role in aging process and that higher intake of them may accelerate aging. Therefore, the dietary intake of some essential minerals competitive against toxic metals, such as zinc, calcium, magnesium and selenium, may be useful for detoxification and controlling aging [31]. Further understanding of molecular and cellular mechanisms of aging could not only improve medical care of the elderly but also hold out some hope in finding feasible solutions to slow down the aging process.

Conclusion

This study demonstrates that toxic metals are classified into two families on the basis of their accumulation profiles in scalp hair specimen. The first family consisting of mercury and arsenic exhibits a characteristic accumulation profile with a marked age-dependency and gender-difference (male > female) in adults. The second family consisting of cadmium, lead and aluminium exhibits a common accumulation profile with the highest burden level in infants, although cadmium has also another character accumulating in aged females, with gender difference (female > male) and age-dependency. These findings suggest that mercury, arsenic and cadmium may be associated with aging, and that higher burden with these toxic metals may lead to acceleration of aging in human.

Acknowledgements

The authors thank the examined subjects for their cooperation to this study.

This study has proceeded for public human health and been supported by La Belle Vie Inc.

References

[1] Harada M. Minamata disease: methylmercury poisoning in Japan caused by environmental pollution. Crit Rev Toxicol 1995; 25: 1- 24.

[2] Chlopicka J, Zachwieja Z, Zagrodzki P, Frydrych J, Slota P and Krosniak M. Lead and cadmium in the hair and blood of children from a highly industrial area in Poland. Biol Trace Elem Res 1998; 62: 229-34.

[3] Sanna E, Liguori A, Palmas L, Soro MR and Floris G. Blood and hair lead levels in boys and girls living in two Sardinian towns at different risks of lead pollution. Ecotoxicol Environ Saf 2003; 55: 293-9.

[4] Samanta G, Sharma R, Roychowdhury T and Chakraborti D. Arsenic and other elements in hair, nails, and skin-scales of arsenic victims in West Bengal, India. Sci Total Environ 2004; 326: 33-47.

[5] Suzuki T, Hongo T, Yoshinaga J, Imai H, Nakazawa M, Matsuo N, *et al.* The hair-organ relationship in mercury concentration in con- temporary Japanese. Arch Environ Health 1993; 48: 221-9.

[6] Yasutake A, Matsumoto M, Yamaguchi M and Hachiya N. Current hair mercury levels in Japanese: Survey in five districts. Tohoku J Exp Med 2003; 199: 161-9.

[7] Goulle JP, Mahieu L, Castermant J, Neveu N, Bonneau L, Laine G, *et al.* Metal and metalloid multi-elementary ICP-MS validation in whole blood, plasma, urine and hair: Reference values. Forens Sci Intern 2005; 153: 39-44.

[8] Munakata M, Onuma A, Haginoya K, Kobayashi Y, Yokoyama H, Fujiwara I, *et al.* Reduced exposure to mercury in patients receiving enteral nutrition. Tohoku J Exp Med 2006; 210: 209-12.

[9] Wang CT, Chang WT, Zeng WF and Lin CH. Concentrations of calcium, copper, iron, magnesium, potassium, sodium and zinc in adult female hair with different body mass indexes in Taiwan. Clin Chem Lab Med 2005; 43: 389-93.

[10] Yasuda H, Yonashiro T, Yoshida K, Ishii T and Tsutsui T. Mineral imbalance in children with autistic disorders. Biomed Res Trace Elem 2005; 16: 285-91.

[11] Yasuda H, Yonashiro T, Yoshida K, Ishii T and Tsutsui T. Relationship between body mass index and minerals in male Japanese adults. Biomed Res Trace Elem 2006; 17: 316-21.

[12] Yasuda H, Yoshida K, Segawa M, Tokuda R, Tsutsui T, Yasuda Y, *et al.* Metallomics study using hair mineral analysis and multiple logistic regression analysis: relationship between cancer and minerals. Environ Health Prev Med 2009; 14: 261-6.

[13] Cranton EM, Bland JS, Chatt A, Krakovitz R and Wright JV. Standardization and interpretation of human hair for elemental concentrations. J Holistic Med 1982; 4: 10-20.

[14] Yasuda H, Yonashiro T, Yoshida K, Ishii T and Tsutsui T. High toxic metal levels in scalp hair of infants and children. Biomed Res Trace Elem 2005; 16: 39-45.

[15] Hirayama K, Yasutake A and Inoue M. Effect of sex hormones on the fate of methyl-mercury and glutathione metabolism in mice. Biochem Pharmacol 1987; 36: 1919-24.

[16] Yamamoto R and Suzuki T. Effects of artificial hair waving on hair mercury values. Int Arch Occup Environ Health 1978; 42: 1-9.

[17] Johnson MD, Kenney N, Stoica A, Hilakivi-Clarke L, Singh B, Chepko G, *et al.* Cadmium mimics the *in vivo* effects of estrogen in the uterus and mammary gland. Nature Med 2003; 9: 1081-4.

[18] Nogawa K, Ishizaki A, Fukushima M, Shibata I and Hagino N. Studies on the women with acquired Fanconi syndrome observed in the Ichi River basin – Is this Itai-itai disease? Environ Res 1975; 10: 280-307.

[19] Fukushima M, Ishizaki A, Sakamoto M, Nogawa K and Kobayashi E. Epidemiological studies on renal failure of inhabitants in “Itai-itai” disease endemic district (Part 2) Observations on urinary abnormalities and cadmium excretion of the inhabitants selected for the close examination of “Itai-itai” disease. Jap J Public Health 1975; 22: 217-224 (in Japanese).

[20] Salonen JT, Seppanen K, Lakka TA, Salonen R and Kaplan GA. Mercury accumulation and accelerated progression of carotid atherosclerosis: a population-based prospective 4-year follow-up study in men in eastern Finland. Atherosclerosis 2000; 148: 265-273.

[21] Guallar E, Sanz-Gallardo MI, van’t Veer P, Bode P, Aro A, Gomez-Aracena J *et al.* Mercury, fish oils, and the risk of myocardial infarction. N Engl J Med 2002; 347: 1747-1754.

[22] Virtanen JK, Voutilainen S, Rissanen TH, Mursu J, Tuomainen TP, Korhonen MJ *et al.* Mercury, fish oils, and risk of acute coronary events and cardiovascular disease, coronary heart disease, and all- cause mortality in men in eastern Finland.

Arterioscler Thromb Vasc Biol 2005; 25: 228-233.

[23] Ziegler EE, Edwards BB, Jensen RL, Mahaffey KR and Fomon SJ. Absorption and retention of lead by infants. Pediatr Res 1978; 12: 29-34.

[24] Freundlich M, Zilleruelo G, Abitbol C, Strauss J, Faugere MC and Mallunche HH. Infant formula as a cause of aluminium toxicity in neonatal uraemia. Lancet 1985; II (8454): 527-9.

[25] Exley C, Begum A, Woolley MP and Bloor RN. Aluminum in tobacco and cannabis and smoking-related disease. Am J Med 2006; 119: 276 e9-e11.Hellstrome HO, Mjoberg B, Mallmin H and Michaelsson K. The aluminium content of bone increases with age, but is not higher in hip fracture cases with and without dementia compared to controls. Osteopor Int 2005; 16: 1982-8.

[26] Mutti A, Corradi M, Goldoni M, Vettori MV, Bernard A and Apos- tori P. Exhaled metallic elements and serum pneumo-proteins in asymptomatic smokers and patients with COPD or asthma. Chest 2006; 129: 1288-97.

[27] Symanski E and Hertz-Picciotto I. Blood lead levels in relation to menopause, smoking, and pregnancy history. Am J Epidemiol 1995; 141: 1047-58.

[28] Gulson BL, Jameson CW, Mahaffey KR, Mizon KJ, Korsch MJ and Vimpani G. Pregnancy increases mobilization of lead from ma- ternal skeleton. J Lab Clin Med 1997; 130: 51-62.

[29] Razagui IB and Ghribi I. Maternal and neonatal scalp hair concentrations of zinc, cadmium, and lead: relationship to some lifestyle factors. Biol Trace Elem Res 2005; 106: 1-28.

[30] Yasuda H, Yoshida K, Fukuchi K, Tokuda R, Tsutsui T and Yonei Y. Association of aging with minerals in male Japanese adults. Anti-aging Med 2007; 4: 38-42.

Chapter 7:

INFANTS AND ELDERLIES ARE SUSCEPTIBLE TO ZINC DEFICIENCY

published in **Scientific Reports 6: 21850 (2016).**

Hiroshi Yasuda and Toyoharu Tsutsui
La Belle Vie Research Laboratory, Tokyo 103-0006, Japan.

Abstract: The importance of zinc for human health has been recognized since the early 1960s, but today there is little concern about zinc deficiency in developed countries. In this study, we measured the zinc concentration in hair from 28,424 Japanese subjects (18,812 females and 9,612 males) and found that 1,754 subjects (6.17%) had zinc concentrations lower than 2 standard deviations (86.3 ppm) below the control reference range, which qualifies as zinc deficiency. In particular, a considerable proportion of elderlies and children (20% or more) were found to have marginal to severe zinc deficiency. A zinc concentration of 9.7 ppm was the lowest observed in a 51-year-old woman; this concentration was approximately 1/13 of the mean reference level. The prevalence of zinc deficiency in adults increased with aging to a maximum of 19.7% by the 8th decade of life, and decreased to 3.4% above 90-year-old. The proportion of zinc deficiency in infants 0–4 years was 36.5% in males and 47.3% in females; these percentages were higher than the maximum prevalence in elderly subjects. These findings suggest that infants and elderlies are prone to zinc deficiency and that intervention of zinc deficiency is necessary for normal human development, health and longevity.

The importance of zinc for human health has been recognized since the early 1960s[1,2]. Zinc is an essential micro- nutrient required for the activity of more than 300 enzymes and 1,000 transcription factors and for the control of genetic expression. It also plays important roles in nucleic acid/protein synthesis, cell replication, and tissue growth and repair[1-4]. Zinc deficiency is known to be associated with various pathological conditions, including impaired immunity, delayed wound healing, retarded growth, neural development disorders and degenerative diseases[1,4].

The use of serum samples alone to assess zinc nutritional status has limitations because serum zinc levels are influenced by factors other than dietary zinc intake, including hypoalbuminemia, infection, acute stress, pregnancy and the use of oral contraceptive agents, all of which can lower serum zinc levels. In addition, serum zinc levels are subject to diurnal variation and are influenced by the fasting status of subjects[5]. Serum zinc levels can be normal even in states of mild deficiency because zinc works primarily as an intracellular nutrient[6,7].

Recent advances in highly sensitive and reliable trace element analysis methods using inductively coupled plasma mass spectrometry (ICP-MS) have enabled the detection of chronic essential mineral deficiencies in the human body. These analyses have shown that human whole blood mineral concentrations are reflected in hair and nail specimens[8,9]. Thus, clinical metallomics studies with reliable ICP-MS methods have been used to investigate the association of several diseases and symptoms with the dynamics of trace bio-elements including toxic metals and essential minerals[10-20].

In this cohort study investigating zinc deficiency, we examined human scalp hair zinc concentrations in 28,424 Japanese subjects with ages ranging from 0 to 100 years.

Results

We measured hair zinc concentrations in 28,424 Japanese subjects (18,812 females and 9,612 males) aged 0-100 years (Fig. 1). The log of the zinc concentration was normally distributed with tailing in the lower range. A total of 1,754 of the 28,424 subjects (6.17%) were found to have zinc concentrations lower than 2 standard deviations (S.D.) below the control reference range (86.3-193 μg/g hair (ppm); geometric mean = 129 ppm), which is considered zinc deficiency (Fig. 2). The lowest zinc concentration measured was 9.69 ppm and was detected in a 51-year-old woman; this concentration corresponded to approximately 1/13 of the mean reference level.

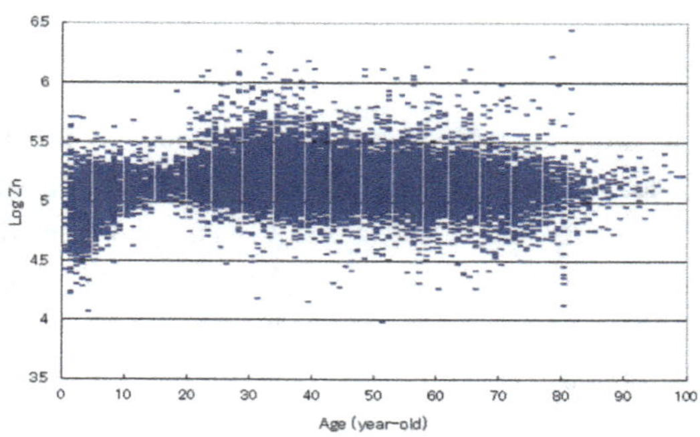

Figure 1. Relationship between hair zinc concentration and age in 28,424 Japanese subjects.

The association between the log of hair zinc concentration and age in Japanese subjects aged 0–100 years (N = 28,424) is shown. Each point represents the corresponding age and log of zinc concentration for the respective subject. The ordinate indicates the log of hair zinc concentration (ng/g hair: ppb).

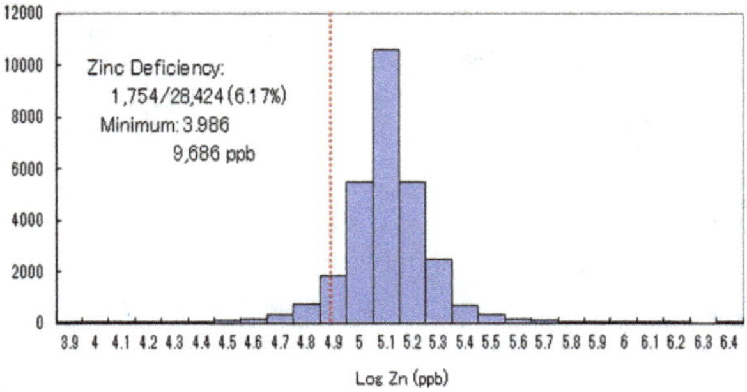

Figure 2. Histogram of log zinc concentration in Japanese subjects (N = 28,424). Hair zinc concentrations for 28,424 subjects are shown in the log plot. The numbers on the abscissa indicate the log of hair zinc concentrations (ng/g hair: ppb). The height of each rectangle represents the frequency in the respective class interval of the log of hair zinc concentration. The dotted vertical line represents the −2 S.D. (standard deviation) level of the control reference range for hair zinc concentrations.

The prevalence of zinc deficiency in the adult male group increased with aging, and when assessed by decade it ranged from 2.0% at the 2nd decade to 4.2, 6.0, 9.7, 11.6% and reached 15.1% by the 7th decade; the rate then decreased to 9.3% or less for ages over 80 years (Fig. 3).

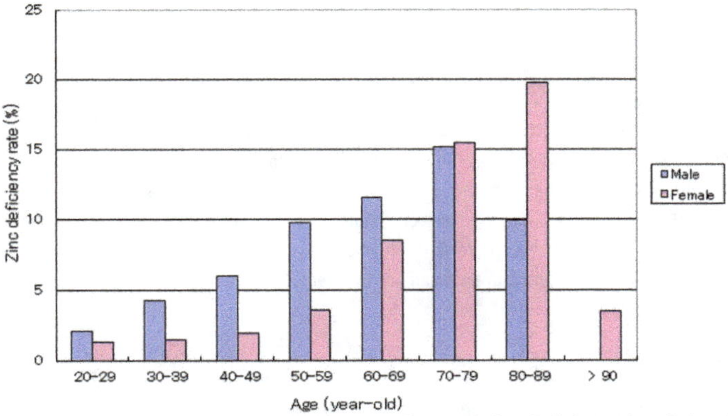

Figure 3. Age-related increase in prevalence of zinc deficiency in adult subjects. The association of zinc deficiency rate with age group (20–100 years old) in adult subjects (N = 25,500) is shown. The height of each rectangle represents the rate of zinc deficiency in the respective age group. The ordinate indicates the zinc

deficiency rate (%).

The zinc deficiency rate in the adult female group also increased by decade from 1.3% at the 2nd decade to 1.5, 1.9, 3.6, 8.5, 15.4% and reached a maximum of 19.7% by the 8th decade; it then decreased to 3.4% for ages above 90 years (Fig. 3). A significant ($p < 0.001$) inverse correlation between the log of the zinc concentration and age ($r = -0.12$ and -0.14 for male and female groups, respectively) was observed (Fig. 4 A, B).

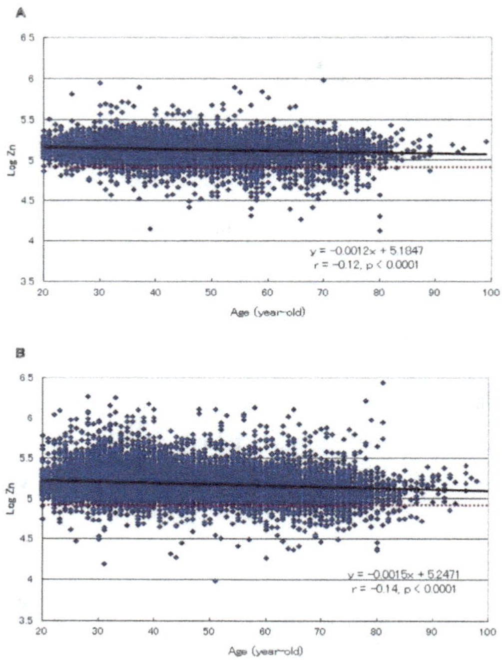

Figure 4. Relationship between zinc concentration and age in male (A) and female (B) adults.
The association of the log of hair zinc concentration with age in male (N = 7,509) and female (N = 17,991) adults aged 20-100 years is shown. Each point represents the corresponding age and log of zinc concentration of the respective subject. The ordinate indicates the log of hair zinc concentration (ng/g hair: ppb). The dotted horizontal line represents the -2 S.D. (standard deviation) level of the control reference range for hair zinc concentrations. A significant inverse relationship between hair zinc concentration and age in the male (**A**) and female (**B**) adults is shown ($r = -0.12$ and -0.14, respectively, $p < 0.0001$).

The prevalence of zinc deficiency in the male and female groups of children aged 0–9 years was 29.9% and 33.8%, respectively; these rates were both higher than the maximum of 19.7% observed in the adult groups. In particular, in infants aged 0-4 years, the prevalence of zinc deficiency was 36.5 and 47.3% in males and females, respectively, and higher rates, over 50%, were observed in the age group including 2- and 3-year-old (Fig. 5). In addition, a highly significant correlation between the zinc concentration and age was observed in the child group ($r = 0.298$, $p < 0.0001$), with a plateau at ages over 10 years (Fig. 6). These findings indicate that infants are more prone to zinc deficiency than elderly individuals, which suggests that an early intervention to correct zinc deficiency is necessary for normal child development and health.

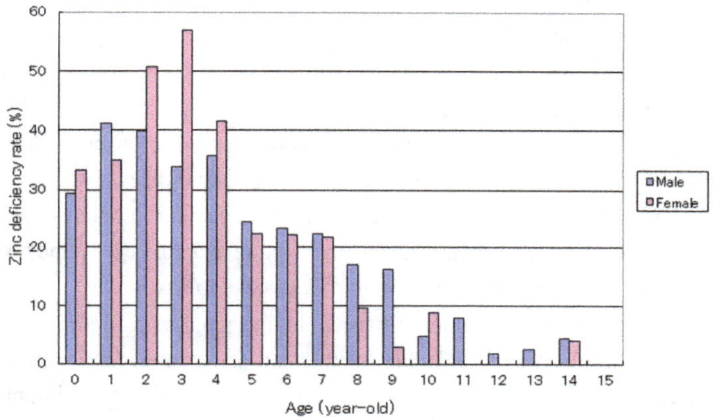

Figure 5. Age-related zinc deficiency rate in children aged 0–15 years.
The incidence of zinc deficiency in every age group is shown for 2,685 children (1,998 males and 687 females) aged 0-15 years. The height of each rectangle represents the rate of zinc deficiency in the respective age group.

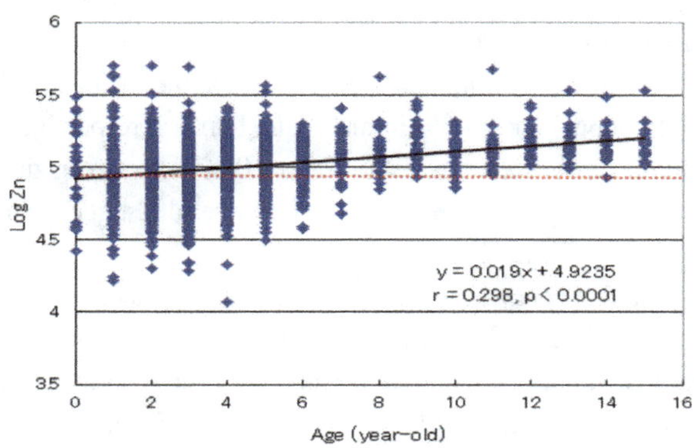

Figure 6. Relationship between zinc concentration and age in children.
The association of the log of hair zinc concentration with age in children aged 0–15 years (N = 2,685) is shown. Each point represents the corresponding age and log of zinc concentration in the respective

subject. The dotted horizontal line represents the −2 S.D. (standard deviation) level of the control reference range for hair zinc concentrations. A significant correlation between the log of zinc concentrations and age was observed in the children ($r = 0.298$, $p < 0.0001$).

Discussion

The importance of zinc in human nutrition and health has been recognized since the early 1960s[1,2]. Because zinc is required for the synthesis and repair of DNA, RNA and proteins, this micronutrient appears to affect the basic biochemical and physiological processes involved in cell growth, cell division, cell differentiation, development and aging[1-4]. Clinical signs of zinc deficiency include acrodermatitis, suppressed immunity, diarrhea, poor healing, stunted growth, hypogonadism, fetal growth failure, teratogenesis and abortion. Zinc deficiency is also known to be associated with various diseases such as malabsorption syndrome, chronic liver disease, chronic renal disease, sickle cell disease, diabetes, malignancy, neurodevelopment disorders and other chronic illnesses[1-4,18-22]. Zinc deficiency also causes significant impairment in adaptive and innate immune responses and promotes systemic immune dysfunction in older populations[2,4,7,23-26].

Hair zinc concentration is commonly used in marginal zinc deficiency studies of children, and its usefulness has been documented in many industrialized countries including Canada and the USA[27-31]. Symptomatic zinc deficiency in infants was first reported in the early 1980s, with most cases occurring in breast-fed preterm infants[32-35] because the zinc concentration of human milk is much lower than that of cow's milk, and the demand for zinc increases rapidly in thriving preterm infants[36].

In the present epidemiological study of 28,424 Japanese subjects, we demonstrated that the prevalence of zinc deficiency in infants is higher than that in adult and elderly subjects. In children aged 0–9 years, nearly one-third (male: 29.9%; female: 33.8%) of the subjects exhibited marginal to severe zinc deficiency. In infants aged 0–4 years, the incidence of zinc deficiency was particularly high: 36.5 and 47.3% in males and females, respectively (Fig. 5). Furthermore, a highly significant correlation ($r = 0.298$, $p < 0.0001$) between zinc concentration and age was observed in these children (Fig. 6). These results suggest that children, particularly infants, are susceptible to zinc deficiency.

The mechanisms that lead to zinc deficiency in infants may include unbalanced meals, lower absorption ability in the intestinal tract[37,38], and low zinc concentration in maternal breast milk[39]. In addition, maternal dieting and cigarette smoking have been reported to be associated with lower zinc and higher cadmium and lead concentrations in neonates[40]. Toxic metals that have accumulated in the maternal bone matrix appear to be co-transferred with calcium and magnesium to fetuses and neonates through accelerated bone-resorption during pregnancy and lactation[40–42].

Severe zinc deficiency in the rare inherited human disease acrodermatitis enteropathica has been reported to result from defective intestinal absorption of zinc due to mutations in the Zip4 transporter located in the intestinal tract[43,44]. Furthermore, recent genetic studies have indicated that mutations in the ZnT2 transporter gene in mothers produce zinc-deficient milk and cause breast-fed infants to develop a severe zinc deficiency[45–47] that can be reversed by zinc replacement therapy[47]. These genetic factors, as well as various environmental factors, also contribute to some zinc deficiencies in infants.

In adults, highly significant ($p < 0.001$) inverse correlations between zinc concentration and age ($r = -0.12$ for males and -0.14 for females) were observed (Fig. 4A, B). In addition, a significant age-dependent increase in the prevalence of zinc deficiency was observed in males and females: from 2.0% to 15.1% by the 7th decade of life and from 1.3% to 19.7% by the 8th decade of life, respectively (Fig. 3). A study conducted in five European countries reported zinc deficiency in 31% of people over 60 years of age, with some country-specific differences in prevalence[48]. Another study of hospitalized elderly patients reported 28% zinc deficiency[49]. These findings indicate that elderly individuals are prone to zinc deficiency, even in developed countries.

It is interesting that male subjects over 85-years-old and females over 90 years old exhibited a low prevalence of zinc deficiency: 3.4% or less (Fig. 3). This finding that zinc deficiency is rare in the older age groups in both genders suggests that the mineral is essential for healthy aging and longevity and that zinc supplementation is probably effective and necessary for aging well.

Recently, dietary-restriction-induced zinc deficiency has been reported to up-regulate the intestinal zinc-importer (Zip4) and induce an increase in Zip4 protein present on the plasma membrane of enterocytes[50]. This adaptive response to zinc deficiency is known to increase the risk of high-uptake of toxic metals such as cadmium and lead. Thus, individuals with zinc deficiency are likely at an increased risk of absorbing large amounts of toxic metals and retaining them in their bodies. In fact, we have demonstrated a highly significant inverse relationship between hair zinc concentration and lead or cadmium concentration[20]. Thus, not only zinc deficiency itself but also the consequent increased risk of toxic metal burden seem to induce various physical and mental disorders[18–21,51,52].

In conclusion, the present study of 28,424 Japanese subjects demonstrates that many cases of zinc deficiency are detected in infants and elderly individuals, indicating that these populations are prone to zinc deficiency. It remains to be established whether early intervention to correct zinc deficiency leads to normal development and health and to healthy aging and longevity.

Methods

Sampling and zinc analysis. After obtaining informed consent, scalp hair samples from 28,424 (male: 9,612; female: 18,812) subjects aged 0–100 years were collected from June 2005 to September 2007 (Table 1). Hair sampling was conducted by cutting hair as close as possible to the scalp of the occipital area.

Age (years)	Female	Male
0–3	200	660
4–9	306	1,000
10–15	181	338
16–19	134	105
20–29	2,817	927
30–39	6,421	2,147
40–49	3,763	1,829
50–59	2,648	1,371
60–69	1,476	796
70–79	695	364
80–	171	75
Total	18,812	9,612

Table 1. Tested Japanese subjects (N = 28,424).

A 75 mg hair sample was weighed into a 50 ml plastic tube and washed with acetone and then with a 0.01% Triton solution, in accordance with the procedures recommended by the Hair Analysis Standardization Board. The washed hair sample was mixed with 10 ml 6.25% tetra methyl ammonium hydroxide (TMAH, Tama Chemical, Kawasaki, Japan) and 50 μL 0.1% gold solution (SPEX Certi Prep, Metuchen, NJ, USA), and then dissolved at 75 C with shaking for 2 hours. After cooling the solution to room temperature, an internal standard solution was added. After adjusting its volume gravimetrically, the obtained solution was used for zinc analysis. The zinc concentrations were determined with inductively coupled plasma mass spectrometry (ICP-MS; 7500ce, Agilent Technologies, Santa Clara, CA, USA) by the internal standard method and expressed as ng/g hair (ppb) or μg/g (ppm) [18,19].

The ethical committee of the La Belle Vie research laboratory reviewed and approved this study. The methods were carried out in "accordance" with the approved guidelines. Informed consent was obtained from all subjects. All of the data collected were held securely in such a form as to ensure anonymity.

Statistical analysis. Because scalp hair mineral concentration follows a log-normal distribution, the log of the zinc concentration and the geometric rather than arithmetic mean were used to represent the hair zinc concentration. The relationship between age and zinc concentration was examined using Pearson's correlation coefficient.

References

1. Prasad, A. S. Zinc: an overview. *Nutrition* **11**, 93–99 (1995).
2. Prasad, A. S. Discovery of human zinc deficiency: Its impact on human health and disease. *Adv. Nutr.* **4,** 176–190 (2013).
3. MacDonald, R. S. The role of zinc in growth and cell proliferation. *Am. Soc. Nutr. Sci.* **130,** 1500S–1508S (2000).
4. Fukada, T., Yamasaki, S., Nishida, K., Murakami, M. & Hirano, T. Zinc homeostasis and signaling in health and diseases. *J. Biol. Inorg. Chem.* **16,** 1123–1134 (2011).
5. Pilch, S. M. & Senti, F. R. Analysis of zinc data from the second national health and nutrition examination survey (NHANES II). *J. Nutr.* **115,** 1393–1397 (1985).
6. Bales, C. W. *et al.* Marginal zinc deficiency in older adults: responsiveness of zinc status indicators. *J. Am. Coll. Nutr.* **13,** 455–462 (1994).
7. Salguairo, M. J. *et al.* Zinc status and immune system relationship: a review. *Biol. Trace Elem. Res.* **71,** 193–205 (2000).
8. Rodushkin, I. & Axelsson, M. D. Application of double focusing sector field ICP-MS for multi elemental characterization of human hair and nails. Part 1. Analytical methodology. *Sci. Total Environ.* **250,** 83–100 (2000).
9. Goulle, J. P. *et al.* Metal and metalloid multi-elementary ICP-MS validation in whole blood, plasma, urine and hair: Reference values. *Forens. Sci. Intern.* **153,** 39–44 (2005).
10. Yasuda, H., Yonashiro, T., Yoshida, K., Ishii, T. & Tsutsui, T. Mineral imbalance in children with autistic disorders. *Biomed. Res. Trace Elem.* **16,** 285–291 (2005).
11. Wang, C. T., Chang, W. T., Zeng, W. F. & Lin, C. H. Concentrations of calcium, copper, iron, magnesium, potassium, sodium and zinc in adult female hair with different body mass indexes in Taiwan. *Clin. Chem. Lab. Med.* **43,** 389–393 (2005).
12. Yasuda, H., Yonashiro, T., Yoshida, K., Ishii, T. & Tsutsui, T. Relationship between body mass index and minerals in male Japanese adults. *Biomed. Res. Trace Elem.* **17,** 316–321 (2006).
13. Munakata, M. *et al.* A preliminary analysis of trace elements in the scalp hair of patients with severe motor disabilities receiving enteral nutrition. *Brain Development* **28,** 521–525 (2006).
14. Adams, J. B., Holloway, C. E., George, F. & Quig, D. Analyses of toxic metals and essential minerals in the hair of Arizona children with autism and associated conditions, and their mothers. *Biol. Trace Elem. Res.* **110,** 193–209 (2006).
15. Yasuda, H. *et al.* Metallomics study using hair mineral analysis and multiple logistic

regression analysis: relationship between cancer and minerals. *Environ. Health Prev. Med.* **14,** 261–266 (2009).

16. Ochi, A. *et al.* Trace elements in the hair of hemodialysis patients. *Biol. Trace Elem. Res*. **143,** 825–834 (2011).

17. Yasuda, H., Yoshida, K., Yasuda, Y. & Tsutsui, T. Two age-related accumulation profiles of toxic metals. *Cur. Aging Sci.* **5,** 105–111 (2012).

18. Yasuda, H., Yoshida, K., Yasuda, Y. & Tsutsui, T. Infantile zinc deficiency: Association with autism spectrum disorders. *Sci. Rep.* **1,** srep00129 (2011).

19. Yasuda, H., Yasuda, Y. & Tsutsui, T. Estimation of autistic children by metallomics analysis. *Sci. Rep.* **3,** srep01199 (2013).

20. Yasuda, H. & Tsutsui, T. Assessment of infantile mineral imbalances in autism spectrum disorders (ASDs). *Int. J. Environ. Res. Public Health* **10,** 6027–6043 (2013).

21. Grabrucker, A. M. Environmental factors in autism. *Front. Psychiatry.* **3,** e118 (2013).

22. Rossignol, D. A., Genuis, S. J. & Frye, R. E. Environmental toxicants and autism spectrum disorders. A systematic review. *Transl. Psychiatry* **4,** e360 (2014).

23. Kitamura, H. *et al.* Toll-like receptor-mediated regulation of zinc homeostasis influences dendritic cell function. *Nat. Immunol,* **7,** 971–977 (2006).

24. Yamasaki, S. *et al.* Zinc is a novel intracellular second messenger. *J. Cell Biol.* **177,** 637–645 (2007).

25. Kawamura, T. *et al.* Severe dermatitis with loss of epidermal Langerhans cells in human and mouse zinc deficiency. *J. Clin. Invest.* **122,** 722–732 (2012).

26. Hojyo, S. *et al.* Zinc transporter SLC39A10/ZIP10 controls humoral immunity by modulating B cell receptor signal strength. *Proc. Natl. Acad. Sci.* **111,** 11786–11791 (2014).

27. Gibson, R. S. *et al.* Growth-limiting, mild zinc-deficiency syndrome in some southern Ontario boys with low height percentiles. *Am.J. Clin. Nutr.* **49,** 1266–1273 (1989).

28. Walravens, P. A., Krebs, N. F. & Hambidge, K. M. Linear growth of low income preschool children receiving a zinc supplement. *Am. J. Clin. Nutr.* **38,** 195–201 (1983).

29. Gibson, R. S. Assessment of trace element status in humans. *Prog. Food Nutr. Sci.* **13,** 67–111 (1989).

30. Vaghri, Z., Barr, S., Wong, H., Chapman, G. & Hertzman, C. Age-based differences in hair zinc of Vancouver preschoolers. *Biol. Trace Elem. Res.* **126,** S21–S30 (2008).

31. Vaghri, Z., Wong, H., Barr, S., Chapman, G. & Hertzman, C. Associations of socio-demographic and behavioural variables with hair zinc of Vancouver preschoolers. *Biol. Trace Elem. Res.* **129,** (2011) PMID: 21369714.

32. Aggett, P. J. *et al.* Symptomatic zinc deficiency in a breast-fed preterm infant. *Arch. Dis. Child.* **55.** 547–550 (1980).

33. Zimmerman, A. W. *et al.* Acrodermatitis in breast-fed premature infants: Evidence for a defect of mammary zinc secretion. *Pediatrics* **69.** 176–183 (1982).

34. Kiechl-Kohlendorfer, U., Fink, F. M. & Steichen-Gersdorf, E. Transient symptomatic zinc deficiency in a breast-fed preterm infant. *Pediatr. Dermatol.* **24,** 536–540 (2007).

35. Barbarot, S. *et al.* Symptomatic acquired zinc deficiency in at-risk premature infants: High dose preventive supplementation is necessary. *Pediatr. Dermatol.* **27,** 380–383 (2010).

36. Kienast, A., Roth, B., Bossier, C., Hojabri, C. & Hoeger, P. H. Zinc-deficiency dermatitis in breast-fed infants. *Eur. J. Pediatr.* **166,** 189–194 (2007).

37. Adams, J. B., Johansen, L. J., Powell, L. D., Quig, D. & Rubin, R. A. Gastrointestinal flora and gastrointestinal status in children with autism – comparisons to typical children and correlation with autism severity. *BMC Gastroenterology* **11,** 22–34 (2011).

38. Dodig-Curkovic, K., Dovhanj, J., Curkovic, M., Dodig-Radic, J. & Degmecic, D. The role of zinc in the treatment of hyperactivity disorder in children. *Acta Med. Croatia* **63,** 307–313 (2009).

39. Ezaki, S., Ito, T., Suzuki, K. & Tamura, M. Association between total antioxidant capacity in breast milk and postnatal age in days in premature infants. *J. Clin. Biochem. Nutr.* **42,** 133–137 (2008).

40. Razagui, I. B. & Ghribi, I. Maternal and neonatal scalp hair concentrations of zinc, cadmium and lead: relationship to some lifestyle factors. *Biol. Trace Elem. Res.* **106,** 1–28 (2005).

41. Symansky, E. & Herz-Picciotto, I. Blood lead levels in relation to menopause, smoking, and pregnancy history. *Am. J. Epidemiol.* **141,** 1047–1058 (1995).

42. Gulson, B. L. *et al.* Pregnancy increases mobilization of lead from maternal skeleton. *J. Lab. Clin. Med.* **130,** 51–62 (1997).

43. Wang, K., Zhou, B., Kuo, Y., Zemansky, J. & Gitschier, J. A novel member of a zinc transporter family is defective in acrodermatitis enteropathica. *Am. J. Hum. Genet.* **71,** 66–73 (2002).

44. Dufner-Beattie, J. *et al.* The acrodermatitis enteropathica gene ZIP4 encodes a tissue-specific, zinc-regulated zinc transporter in mice. *J. Biol. Chem.* **278,** 33474–33481 (2003).

45. Chowanadisai, W., Lonnerdal, B. & Kelleher, S. L. Identification of a mutation in SLC30A2 (ZnT-2) in women with low milk zinc concentration that results in transient

neonatal zinc deficiency. *J. Biol. Chem.* **281,** 39699–39707 (2006).

46. Lasry, I. *et al.* A dominant negative heterozygous G87R mutation in the zinc transporter, ZnT-2 (SLC30A2), results in transient neonatal zinc deficiency. *J. Biol. Chem.* **287,** 29348–29361 (2012).

47. Itsumura, N. *et al.* Compound heterozygous mutations in SLC30A2/ZnT2 results in low milk zinc concentrations: A novel mechanism for zinc deficiency in a breast-fed infant. *PLoS ONE* **8,** e64045 (2013).

48. Marcellini, F., *et al.* Zinc status, psychological and nutritional assessment in old people recruited in five European countries: Zinc age study. *Biogerontrogy* **7,** 339–345 (2006).

49. Pepersack T. *et al.* Prevalence of zinc deficiency and its clinical relevance among hospitalized elderly. *Arch. Gerontol. Geriatr.* **33,** 243–253 (2001).

50. Cousins, R. J., Liuzzi, J. P. & Lichten, L. A. Mammalian zinc transport, trafficking, and signals. *J. Biol. Chem.* **281,** 24085–24089 (2006).

51. Gronli, O., Kvamme, J. M., Friborg, O. & Wynn, R. Zinc deficiency is common in several psychiatric disorders. *PLoS ONE* **8,** e82793 (2013).

52. Swardfager, W. *et al.* Zinc in depression: a meta-analysis. *Biol. Psychiatry* **74,** 872–878 (2013).

Acknowledgements

The authors would like to thank the subjects for their contribution to this study. The authors also thank colleagues who made technical contributions to this study.

Author Contributions

H.Y. performed the experiments, analyzed the data and wrote the manuscript with the help of T.T.

Epilogue

The importance of zinc for human health has been recognized since the early 1960s, but there was little concern about zinc deficiency in developed countries.

The seven research articles collected in this book call attention to the deficiency of restricted two essential minerals "zinc and magnesium" and also to the high burdens of toxic metals such as aluminum, lead, cadmium, and mercury or arsenic, especially in the 0-4 years-old children with neurodevelopmental disorders. Furthermore, it is emphasized that there is a high-significant inverse relationship observed between every high-burdened metal and zinc level in the autistic children, suggesting that zinc element plays crucial role as gatekeeper antagonist against toxic metals' burdens. These findings suggest that zinc and magnesium deficiency and toxic metal burdens in infants and fetus, play critical roles as epigenetic environmental factors, in the pathogenesis of neurodevelopmental disorders such as ASD and ADHD.

In addition, it should be emphasized that there is a critical period named "Infantile Time Window" in the pathogenesis of neurodevelopmental disorders and for the prevention and treatment, suggesting that the early assessment and intervention of the body mineral imbalances in the patients are essential for the prevention/therapy. (Chapter 1-5)

Thus, early screening and assessment of infants and children suffering from essential mineral deficiencies and/or toxic metal burdens would be necessary, and also evidence-based supplementation of the deficit-minerals (e.g. zinc and magnesium) should be considered.

This evidence-based nutritional therapeutic approach, that is, supplementing deficient minerals and detoxifying accumulated toxic metals is of great importance for normal neurodevelopment and growth of infantile children, and probably yields a novel pathway into the prevention/treatment of neurodevelopmental disorders and also comorbid allergic diseases such as atopy, food allergy, asthma and so on.

The two articles (Chapter 6 and 7), for 28,424 Japanese subjects aged 0-100 years old, demonstrate that body zinc levels in adults are decreasing with aging and the burden levels of toxic metals are increasing with aging. These findings indicate that elderlies are susceptible to not only zinc-deficiency but also high burdens of toxic heavy metals, as well as infants.

Furthermore, it is interesting that male subjects over 85-year-old and females over 90 years old exhibited a low prevalence of zinc deficiency of 3.4% or less. This finding that zinc deficiency is rare in the older age groups in both genders suggests that this mineral is essential for healthy aging and longevity and that zinc supplementation is probably effective and necessary for healthy aging. It remains to be established whether early intervention to correct zinc deficiency leads to normal development, wellness and to healthy aging and longevity.

By recent extensive biomedical researches on zinc element and its-deficiency has been increasingly spotlighted in the context of various diseases development and prevention: namely, diabetes, inflammatory bowel disease, immune disorders, infections, neurodevelopmental and neurodegenerative diseases, cancer and so on. In fact, many challenging clinical studies with zinc-supplement or drug, which has been prescribed for the therapy of Wilson disease, have been started for neurodegenerative disorders such as Alzheimer disease, Parkinson disease and amyotrophic lateral sclerosis (ALS).

It is expected that the evidence-based supplementation of deficit minerals such as zinc and magnesium in early phase of aging ameliorates not only body mineral imbalances but also various clinical symptoms related to the deficiencies and toxic metal burdens.

Therefore, we hope that controlled double-blind clinical studies will clarify the epigenetic relationship between a variety of body mineral imbalances and various diseases, providing a reasonable and essential procedures for individualized precision therapy. In the near future, clinical metallomics (or "mineralomics") analysis, with another micronutrient omics "vitaminomics" analysis, will be used as an essential tool for evidence-based personalized precision medicine, leading to healthy life, wellness and longevity.

Acknowledgments:

The author appreciates all of the study subjects for collaboration to these studies. We sincerely hope that the contents of this book contribute to making your lives more comfortable.

I express my gratitude to the collaborators and La Belle Vie Laboratory. Without your presence, these cutting-edge studies would not have been possible.

I also thank my family.
Without their unwavering support and dedication, I would not be able to accomplish anything.

www.ingramcontent.com/pod-product-compliance
Lightning Source LLC
LaVergne TN
LVHW022100200926
848481LV00003B/1010